ALSO BY AMIT MAJMUDAR

POETRY

Dothead

0°, 0°

Heaven and Earth

FICTION

The Abundance

Partitions

Sitayana (India)

Soar (India)

TRANSLATION

Godsong: A Verse Translation of the Bhagavad-Gita, with Commentary

AS EDITOR

Resistance, Rebellion, Life: 50 Poems Now

What He Did in Solitary

What He Did in Solitary

POEMS

Amit Majmudar

ALFRED A. KNOPF   NEW YORK   2020

THIS IS A BORZOI BOOK
PUBLISHED BY ALFRED A. KNOPF

Copyright © 2020 by Amit Majmudar

Library of Congress Cataloging-in-Publication Data
Names: Majmudar, Amit, author.
Title: What he did in solitary : poems / Amit Majmudar.
Description: First edition. | New York : Alfred A. Knopf, 2020. | "This is
a Borzoi book." |
Identifiers: LCCN 2019042972 (print) | LCCN 2019042973 (ebook) |
ISBN 9780525656517 (hardcover) | ISBN 9780525656524 (ebook)
Subjects: LCGFT: Poetry.
Classification: LCC PS3613.A3536 W47 2020 (print) | LCC PS3613.A3536
(ebook) | DDC 811/.6—dc23
LC record available at https://lccn.loc.gov/2019042972
LC ebook record available at https://lccn.loc.gov/2019042973

Jacket image by BirdImages / E+ / Getty Images
Jacket design by John Gall

Manufactured in the United States of America
First Edition

The works, no doubt still serviceable, had not been wound in two centuries. But then again, it was not to tell the time that I had purchased this clock in Touraine.

—GÉRARD DE NERVAL

Contents

What He Did in Solitary

I am no writer. I believe
the I who writes here isn't me.
When the I in me gets up and leaves,
who's writing this? Do I believe
myself the stranger who conceives
my self-estranged identity?
A writer's no one, if you believe
the I who writes here. Is this me?

The Adventures of Amit Majmudar

Never laid a snare for nothin.
Never caught a bullfrog. Broke
my slingshot wishbone, wishin.
Never had a smoke.
Never clipped a baseball card
to thutter in the spokes.
My fist clenched an ink pen
and I learned what to think when
and never swore no *Honest Injun,*
and never spat, and never struck.
Where you gone, Tom?
Where you at, Huck?

I call myself a man today
though I've never been a boy
and dug for treasure in the woods
or lost myself in play
feared dead for seven days
until I showed up by my grave
and made a sniffling town rejoice.
I could have been a pirate, Mama,
at least a Robin Hood,
but I was always up to something
employable and good,
and now I'm down here in this cave,
crying, crying to be saved
though I reckon I am stuck.
Where you gone, Tom?
Where you at, Huck?

Of Age

You've come of age in the age of migrations.
The board tilts, and the bodies roll west.
Fanaticism's come back into fashion,
come back with a vengeance.
In this new country, there's no gravitas,
no grace. The ancient Chevys migrate
west and plunge like maddened buffalo
into a canyon. Where the oil-slick geese go,
no one knows—maybe the Holland Tunnel
because they take it for the monstrous turbine
promised them in prophecy. I brought you
to this world, and I do not regret it.
The sky's still blue, for now. I want to show you
an island where the trees are older than redwoods
ever since Prospero turned them
into books. You'll meet him when you're ready.
For now, though, study this list of endangered
species: It's incomplete, of course, since all
species are in some danger nowadays.
This is the country I bequeath to you,
the country I bequeath you to. You've come
of age, and you're inheriting the whole house,
busted pipes and splintered deck and all.
This is your people, this, the mythic West
your grandparents wished to reach, and reached.
The oceans surge, but the boat is up on blocks.
There's no America to sail to anymore.

Bully

First day fake friend
With the knuckle-
Crusher handshake
Making new kids

Buckle pleading
By the bus stop:
Art Class vandal,
Safety scissors

Leaving jackknife-
Streaks on Andy's
Weekslong van Gogh
(Oddly savvy,

Though, when sneering
Just be glad I
Didn't slash your
Ear off for you):

Rubber cement
Booger-flicker,
Aiming always
At our terror

Eyes: touch-football
Blindside tackler
On the recess
Blacktop, cackling

At my swiftly
Swelling ankle . . .
By some just as
Human impulse,

Paul "the Mauler"
Miller pulled me
Up and crutched me
On his shoulder

To the nurse's
Office; next day,
Called me *shitskin*
Like before; the

Next night, one night
Short of summer,
Hunkered in a
Crawl space while his

Former jarhead
Father rounded
On his family
With a legal

Handgun, starting
At the upstairs
Crib and ending
In the basement,

Sparing only
Two beloved
Dobermans out
Back on choke chains.

Air Jordans

I got my first ones thanks
to my uncle Rishi. Dad
was all, You've got to learn
to see *through* such things, son!
It's all marketing!
But I'd been staring at
that jumpman logo long
enough to see a Darwinian
great leap upward.
Absolute levitation, no line
to indicate the court
or even sea level.
That wasn't a basketball
but another planet's moon
or sun he'd jumped to tag,
to ring the clear sound out of
the way I used to sprint
and launch my twelve-
year-old fingertips
at the little temple bell
while everyone else
chanted and mumbled and knelt
to elevate themselves.
As if the Gods had called me
to jump, boy, jump, boy,
one arm up, one arm
down, like the overreacher
on my sneakers shooting
his body past the hoop
of the horizon.
You're supposed to take off
your shoes before you enter

one of our temples,
but I wouldn't leave the new
Air Jordans that had just
touched down in my life
unattended out there
among ratty old sandals
and scuffed-up loafers.
Either I go in with these on,
I said, or I'll just swish
these prayers from half-court.
After a ten-minute dispute,
I strode in, soles
squeaking, equipped
with the attitude, altitude,
weightlessness I needed
to jump (tongue out)
and get my whole hand
thwang! on that brass bell,
so loud and sharp the assembled
worshippers broke
their solemn show piety
and turned to look
at nerdy me suspended
in that note I'd struck,
one arm down, one arm
up, my skinny legs
flung wide, and at the ends
of them my Jordans
glowing holy
red and white.

Chillicothe Apostrophe

Here's my odi-et-amo
homely Ohio
semis crisscrossing
magnificent buffalo,
under flecked hotlamps,
parlor parking lots
where the whiteboys
and talk black with platinum-
(counties once Ku Klux
your Amish-kitchen
your former fighter
in whose mute dementia
your trickle-crooked creeks
and spanned by rust-
your coal-car carcasses,
shucked of equity,
necrotic Cleveland
equal parts
Youngstown with no young
Painesville painting herself
fought for, fawned over
when donkeys and elephants
stampede your stadiums,
state of the suddenly
and shrunken truckers
of immigrant internists
and cumin-cologned,
with stumps for thumbs,
malls and the algae lake,
cry woe, Cuyahoga, O
maker of Presidents,
O heart shape, O hardship,

Ode to you, O
of the torn-up turnpike,
your map like mudflap-
frankfurters sweating
back-country ice cream
cacophanously Kanye
wear wifebeaters
plated buckteeth
now bling bling),
smoked ham and pancakes,
pilots with Parkinson's
Ashland is Inchon,
once flush, now fishless
rotted struts,
your house husks
to the brambles abandoned,
suburb-encrusted
elegy and punch line,
steel-mill-sepulchral,
Pabst blue, O you,
every four years
(asinine, self-trumpeting)
factories, fairgrounds,
sad-eyed barflies
with saggy tattoos,
soft-spoken
of table-saw grampaws
state of the ghost strip
alas, Ashtabula,
nowhere I am native,
mother of poets,
Ohio, O home.

Owed to Cleveland

City I was always
leaving
but even
now that I live elsewhere
haven't left

City built on iron
and then when iron fell through
on decay

City where the dying
come to stay

Your hospitals gone up
like factories

refining your only
your infinite
natural resource

disease

My dad was one of your diligent
Indian physicians
never letting red lights stop him
not until he saw the floodlit glass
pavilion
floating on the air

over Euclid
& Chester
Kinsman
St. Clair

Coronaries
narrow
traffic to a standstill
on Dead Man's Curve

I saw my first
gunshot wound
to the neck
and then that same afternoon
the left leg of my scrubs

still flecked
stumbled down the street
to see my first
El Greco

To cleave, to stick to something
To cleave, to strike a thing apart

City of scalpels
city of switchblades
designing on the heart

El Greco
how, nobody knows
could render the savior
haggard yet somehow
aglow

To render, to process an animal carcass
To render, to depict in art

Cleveland

Dirty needles
grew dragonfly-wings
and battened on
your flung-wide arms

abscesses seeded
all along

Carnegie Avenue
East 55th
Superior Road

Cleveland my Cleveland
I leave you
this Ode

my beloved
my first
my closest thing to a home

decembering under
the opiate snow

How Do I Say That, Where Is That From

I want a white name,
        But not too white,
A name just white
        Enough, just right,

Not Ebenezer,
        Not Issachar,
Not Mel or Milton,
        Merv or Marv,

Not a white name back
        From way white when
But a half-familiar
        Bleachonym

That will not stain
        Or estrange my books,
A name like Frazier,
        Rouse, or Hooke,

First name to match,
        Your fave, your friend,
Your Jonathan
        Or Dave or Ben,

Its white the white
        Of an egg, or an eye,
A white with nothing
        To imply,

White as a wall
        On which the art
Is noticed from
        The very start,

A name as white
        As the white on a page
That does not draw
        The gaze away,

Dissolving cloudlike
        Overhead
To let the written
        Word be read.

Elmer's Glue

I made things stick by writing a name, flipping it, crushing it flat with a fist. Nicole, Katie, Melissa: names not meant for me. Elmer I imagined as a taciturn farmer, Katie's grandfather maybe out in Coshocton, where he owned this smiling heifer on the label. I squeezed and wrote my secret loves and hid them between two surfaces of different-color construction paper, my art a sealed envelope full of yearning, a bony brown boy's yearning that held together mobiles, dioramas, posters. The orange nipple always clogged at the tip, a little plug I could pick off and flick at Nicole, at Katie, at Melissa, stirring their annoyance because I couldn't stir their desire, anything just to be seen and spoken to. This was the same white I milked from the zits of my teenage years, the same stuff of yearning I still squeeze out to pen my poems about the old crushes I've never forgotten, Nicole, Katie, Melissa, my memory stuck on them, stuck with them, adhering to my old frustrations like a faith, glued to the past with Elmer's glue. I used to hide my fingerprints under its whiteness. I would have poured gloves and worn them for the rest of my childhood, but a false skin always peels away, leaving you with your own hands again. I got used to mine eventually. I write my own name now. As you can see, I air it facing up.

To His Soul

Soul,
You, too, are just another locust,
Only lonely in the swarm,
Soul,
You pagan clinging to this body,
Your rabbit's foot, your charm
Against the death that pricks
Your ears up in alarm,
Soul,
You firecracker hidden in a midden,
You prize in every box,
Soul,
You web designer, working from home
In nothing but your socks
And in that home so scared you spend
Your whole life checking locks,
Soul,
You self-proclaimed sequoia felled
With just a couple thwocks,
Soul,
You, too, are just one more deserter
Haggard, eager to disarm,
Hoping these Americans
Don't mean to do you harm

Vocative

English is my native
anguish. I was born here,
read here, teased and torn here.
Vocative, ablative,

locative, alive:
English was a dislocation
navigating oceans.
Wherever it arrived,

it broke and brokered words,
little bits of Britain
pilfered, bartered, written,
looted, hoarded, heard.

Papa swapped a world
for shiny colored beads,
for dandelion seeds.
We are subject verbs.

The root word of my name
hooks a foreign land,
long-since-shifted sand
books cannot reclaim.

Graft of tongue, gift of dust,
mother and stranger, sing
the kedgeree, the everything
at once you've made of us.

Invasive Species

The bees are Africanized. All elm disease is Dutch.
The carp is Asian, the python of the Everglades
specifically Burmese. The plague bacillus
sailed from India to Europe. Europe coughed
khaki back at India. Everything is alien,
especially starthistle with its spurs and bursts,
unearthly, mapping its home galaxy
like a foundling with a fleur-de-lys foot tattoo.
Though even lilies hitchhike—every ditch lily
was once a tiger lily, treasured in the garden
of a Mughal. Everybody thinks the Mughals
Indian, but *Mughal* comes from *Mongol*.
Invaders make themselves at home and home
remakes them into natives. Everybody comes
from someplace else where they were royal
refugees. We flower where we flower,
flinging roots like ropes from runaway
hot-air balloons to snag a city's skyline.
It never feels like an invasion when
you're doing it. It feels like parenting,
like cooking what you've always cooked, like dancing
with your grandma at a noisy wedding.
But then you turn to see the horrified
park rangers staring at you, calling in
the experts—look at this, what do we do,
they're everywhere. You wonder who they mean,
but then you see. Their poison hemlock? That
is you. Their brown tree snake. Their killer bee.

The Beard

What was I like, before this beard?
More like, what was I *not* like.
Who I was depended.
I feared consensus
because stupidity lies
in numbers.
Among believers an atheist,
among atheists a skeptic,
among skeptics an agnostic,
among agnostics all emphatic
on the apophatic,
I laughed in my beard
at market panics,
fanaticism, Beyoncé worship.
Not that I had a beard back then.
Neither did Ahmad Rahami
on his driver's license,
my doppelgänger Afghan,
mon semblable, I will not say *mon frère.*
When the pictures of him bearded,
beardless, bearded
showed up on sixty million screens,
I was partway through my third mile
on an Urban Active treadmill.
Well shucks, I thought, and yes
that quaint Midwestern word
appears in my internal monologues.
Well shucks, that bastard looks like me.
Judging from the sidelong glances
of flat-footed accountants running
for their lives
to either side of me,

I was not the only one who thought so.
The more they eyed me,
the more my face began to itch.
By mile five, this thing had bushed out,
my face a time-lapse Chia Pet,
and off the treadmill I was running
to my car for dear life
and a Schick Quattro.
I've tried a classic straight razor
I got off Amazon
and a Braun electric shaver, too.
The shave is not so much
not close enough as not
a shave at all, instead a kind
of endless passing of my hand
unbelieving through a hologram.
The more folks look, the more it grows.
You see it's quite foreclosed
the flux of me. I've gone from being
e pluribus unum
(and on that pluribus
every rider
me and me and me)
to maybe him, unknowably.
I try to talk to keep things chummy
because my silence, once the sign
of my interiority,
is now at best a sulk, at worst a seethe,
Ahmad, Amit, Rahimi, him me,
me with no way now to bare
my true face veiled beneath his beard.
I am alone here now,
among Americans a foreigner
when just last year I used to be
among Americans American.

Basketball

Rubber gooseflesh
seamed with black grooves
fingertip-deep:
Growing up,
this was the texture
and shape of my world.
My brown boy's hand
would never grow
big enough to grip one
upside down.
Even now it's magic
to see one stuck
to a level palm,
tucked there like a yo-yo
grabbed on the windup.
Jordan in my daydreams,
I stuck out my bright tongue
on my way to heaven,
but the one I loved most
was Scottie Pippen,
his greatness devoted
to the one greatness
greater than his,
mastery accepting
the diminutive.
I found the old basketball
while cleaning out
the garage for my parents
on the eve of the sale.
My thumbs dented it
into a beggar's bowl.
I slid home the needle's

rescue IV, pumped
my boyhood up again,
chest compressions
on a friend found down.
The surface felt too smooth—
a decade of dribbling,
three more of dust—
but my fingers could reread
its epic poem in Braille
recounting mythical Bulls
that could fly through the air,
of giants with their tongues out
jumped to pluck the sun's
ripe orange from the sky
and dunked it in the sea
every game night,
swinging weightlessly
from the hoop of the horizon.

Rupture is the road to rapture.
Lovers slip on a bridge of rope,
their spasms past, this chasm after
a self made whole and made to rupture.
The self alone, escaping capture,
all by her lonesome laughs and elopes,
riding inward to the rapture
along a bridge of fraying hope.

Bloodline

My great-grandfather married a hurricane,
taking a hold of her whiplash wrist.
She stopped spinning and let him love her,
a wife in her weathers while his parents despaired.
She bore him babies, three at one scream,
then dissolved over land, leaving him dad—
shards and shingles on a mortgaged mile.
Each baby's birthmark was peril and prophecy,
the littlest triplet's a forest fire
branded on her brow. She gobbled boys
like Californias! Coal in her fist
would crush to ravens that knew her name.
How could she not be known and courted
through six counties? My father's father
flung his future in a fistful
of heart-shaped confetti consumed by her hunger.
She bore him a boy with cheeks like
a volcano, wicks twisting out of his navel
in a blasted bouquet, poisoned pistils;
then left him for a lover, an April migrant
picking strawberries, her bronze Apollo
en español. He cut her throat.
My father, when he turned twenty-three, fell
for his mother's memory, a storm with a name,
raven-haired and raving mad.
She kept us cowering, scrambling for cover,
every vacation demanding sandbag
barricades at Marriotts, retreats to the roof.
So now you know my love life's
embarrassingly bad genetic juju—
if you want in on this wicked lineage,
let's sky-write our names in smoke and money

with paper planes
let's bury ourselves
start up a business
in a haze, in heat,

we'll light and launch,
in the burning sand,
on the ill-starred boardwalk,
in hurricane season.

Nostalgia

Once upon a time. Twice, on her parents' bed.
She freaked out when she found the human stain
Dried rough in the rough shape of the male brain.
Cautious ever after, after that she said
She liked it when I shot her in the head.
She blew my brains out. Bang bang, I was dead,
Unarousable there in the first-floor master.
Sometimes, on long drives, she'd gun me. Faster, faster
I tongued the olive pressed between her thighs.
Floaters, she swore, as bright as rescue flares
Would dive across the dark behind her eyes.
I pearl-dove and never once came up for air
There in her aunt's houseboat on Lake Champlain.
The wetter she got the harder I smelled the rain.

Elemental

The sky goes naked. Daylight cannot shame the air.
I try to write your body, but it feels like naming air.
   Inside you: if not as your lover, then your breath.
I became my voice when you became my air.

You are my limit. To your north is fire.
From my balcony I toast the forest fire
   Looting Plumas County by its own light.
One day I'd like to be reborn as fire.

When was the last time my bare feet felt the earth?
Love, I will abase myself. Tell the earth
   I want to fall from high noon and land on your wrist.
I want to die as rain to learn the smell of earth.

If I am dust, then you are seed and sun and water,
Mustard seed and only sun and wonder water
   Working wonders in the deeps of humdrum me.
Hold me, love. If you want to, underwater.

Cat's Cradle

My hands hold
the pattern that
    holds them fast. Your

hands pluck the string
    to make the music
that frees me up

    at last. We lift away
entanglements
    we trade

like tongues. The cat
    in my crèche
is your name

    on my breath. To love
is to be bound
    like this and freed

like this. The pattern
    that weaves my
hands together

    blinks and opens
in your hands,
    a new dreamcatcher

with you the dream
    inside it. Isn't it beautiful
to need like this?

Pattern crisscrosses
pattern, hands
swooping in

to rescue hands.
They never touch
in their mercurial

aerial dance. One loop
of string
strings fate

along with elusively
feline ingenuity,
you and me

in pattern
after pattern
recurring

while our Cheshire love
with its nine lives
and sleepy topaz eyes

lies in its
shapeshifting cradle
purring.

Folding

Tonight, love, let's rush to the trilling dryer
and scoop our strange new clothes into our arms.
The warmth won't last for long, every involved
sleeve a tidepool of heat too soon to drain.
What a blessing this is, to lie back and tumble
a hug's worth of sweatshirts and yoga pants
over our faces and shoulders! To bury each other
in fistfuls of machine-wash-warm spring cloud!
The soaked and soaped, bedraggled undies
spin to lacy congeries of lingerie.
Our coarsest husks go light as cotton candy.
Peek in there, and it's a barrel full of colors
thrust up, swiveling, flailing slack back down
like a bounce house full of comatose clowns.
Forget the basket, love, let's take our clothes
straight from their new womb to our bed and bask
atop our tangled wardrobes for a bit,
letting the warmth pass through our bodies back
into a cosmos that will never notice it.
There will be time enough for spills and seas
to dry, and time for bodies to go threadbare.
And when the bed cools, we'll sit up and sort
yours from mine and mine from yours. After we slant
our sleeves in even V's, and pat the wrinkles
as if a touch will make them go away,
we'll brush the crow's feet from each other's eyes,
lie flat, and fold our arms across our chests.

Neurology of Love

1. Astereognosis

[a loss of the ability to recognize objects by handling them]

Starknowing. He places his hand in hers,
but she doesn't recognize it. What was love once
is beyond forgotten now, is never having known
at all. Astereognosis, agnosis, *No* is
the only word her tongue recognizes
by its shape, four thorns and a nubbin bud.
Hands can forget shapes, and his,
in time, will forget hers—palmblind, unable
to tell her skin from yesterday's breeze.
He closes his eyes, and this weightless edgeless
textureless something in his hands
may well be the night sky
on a planet orbiting
an unknowable star. This feels
unfamiliar, but so does everything,
for both of them. The shape
the silence makes between them
is either a love poem
or a love-poem-shaped goodbye.

2. Apophenia

[the perception of patterns and connections where none exist]

Their minds were rhymes. But rhymes can rhyme by chance.
A rhythm, too, can hear itself where there's
really nothing but the rain's spondees
for the span of a day, the first day
he is alone, she is alone,
symmetrical, without connection.
Stand outside in the rain long enough,
and patter will give way to pattern.
What's a pattern anyway, he wonders,
but the repetition of a mistake?
Fold the sheet in half, and any bloodstain
is a Rorschach butterfly. What
he's done to her he's done to her
again, again, but what it really means is,
he's still in love. Replay
the footage of the burning car.
She's still in love. Reload
her heart's kaleidoscope with shards.

3. Prosopagnosia

[the inability to recognize faces]

The mouth shape recognizably
a mouth, the eye shapes recognizably
two eyes, but seen together,
strange. She never thought she'd call him
a stranger to his face, but now her name
emerging from that mouth shape there
is Greek to her. The ancient tragedies
are always ending with *anagnorisis,*
the recognition scene, in which the lover
proves to be the one person
the oracle warned you never to love.
Might this estrangement be
the least unhappy ending?
The actor has dropped his mask at last,
the reality beneath as unfamiliar
as the night sky over Delphi
riddled with stars
and a moon the face of someone
gazing past her
who even though she's seen him
night after night after night
is no one she knows.

Why an Octopus

Because her nerves, dispersed over her body, made her treat touch as one more form of cognition

Because a male who let himself get too close to her while mating always risked being devoured in some way

Because she could assume the shape of any hollow, whether a solitude, or a martini glass, or a pill bottle, or an exhaust pipe, or an oven

Because she showed behaviors seemingly expressive of human emotions while remaining fundamentally alien

Because she wrapped her innumerable and sentient long legs around me and began to suck

Because she nursed a darkness in her that she spat into a stormcloud of unknowing when she decided to vanish

Because, penetrable everywhere, everywhere depthless, she pulled me in with her vulnerability, a mollusk born without a shell

Because she could squeeze through a hole the size of a wedding ring and emerge on the other side of it unchanged

The Fencing Shoe

Really, with him so young, the kids so young—
his mother (who had never liked his choice)
was waiting out the fall before she asked him.
She had some candidates in mind. So did
the ladies at her book club. They would wait.
But he'd already thought it through that morning
six weeks past the wake when he awoke
alive and hard the first time in forever
and lay there motionless for half an hour
remembering Sir Richard Francis Burton's
favorite fencing shoe, the one he carried
across five continents and Iceland, begging
the cobblers everywhere he traveled
(and Burton traveled *everywhere*) to make
a mate for, since he'd lost the first one back
in Guzerat, when he was twenty-two.
He really *loved* those fencing shoes, the way
the lost one used to hug his leading foot.
The cobbler in Trieste, who could have used
the money, crossed himself and shook his head.
As far off as Harar and Buenos Aires,
in villages a shoelace wide, in *Iceland,*
even, the superstition held: No cobbler
would dare restore the pair. In fact, the word
they used, when pointing at the shoe he showed them,
astonished him, the same in Portuguese,
Amharic, Hindi, Scots, the whisper falling
like fresh snow in Icelandic: *widower.*

Squanderlust

Love is a circle that ends when it ends.
I played the love I never loved so hard.
I returned to my lie, and I told it again.

Remorse revised while deadlines came and went,
While buses burned and onetime allies warred.
Life is a circle that starts as it ends.

My body was a cage where I was pent,
My bare hands holding bloody jaws apart.
I return to the lion and tame it again,

But lust is a hunger only tongues repent,
And lovers stroke the skin where they were scarred,
Circles of pleasure that finish before they end.

I thought that I was better than other men,
That it wasn't cheating, just a false start.
But now love is a race I cannot run again.

I never said exactly what I meant.
Flaws are forgiven less in love than art,
But if loss is a circle that starts where it ends,
I'll return to this line, and I'll write it again.

Solitary Sonzal

Whose voice was that, here, where I lie alone?
Look at you, said Eros. *Scared, shy, alone.*

I dreamt my dreaming of you
Brought us together.

I love you as only dust can love you.
I dreamt us swept up on a gust together.

I alone have vanished. Look above you:
Nothing and nothing, thrust together.

> Breather of secrets,
> Do I sigh alone?

> I fear love. But I fear regret.
> *I made you*, said Eros. *I alone.*

> *Cautious men die old, Amit.*
> *They also die alone.*

Poem Beginning with a Line by Ovid

Of bodies changed to other forms I tell
anybody who will listen. Listen: my uncle Rishi
changed into a blue heron's reflection in water
and stared into the sky until the sun went down
on the day he died. He died of kidney failure—
that was what they said in the announcement
because no one died of AIDS back then, not in our family.
In our family, no one died of anything, just changed
to a different form, wren form, cricket form, koi form
picked up like the end of a sentence swung around
and set down as the start of a sentence. A sentence
in a new language the tongue never twisted to fit before
because sometimes the body that doesn't fit can be a life
sentence, as it was for Uncle Rishi. Uncle Rishi
would have loved to change his form to a woman's
and love a man—in India, in the 1980s, in our family—
but karma says you can switch into another body only
if you die. You die little by little, waiting, Uncle Rishi
on all fours in his lover's flat, lowing at the sky
like a heifer waiting for her milk to come in. To come in
to his old body after that—the flared wingspan
forgotten, forgotten the sweat on the horse's tree-thick neck—
was a comedown, a letdown, solitary confinement
in his form. His form was beautiful, too beautiful
for a boy—our family used to despair
of ever finding a girl to match his long lashes and full lips,
my mom tells me, to this day never saying outright
the truth about her brother. Her brother
became a horse and took the bit in his mouth, became
a flying fish and stole the pleasures of one body
by transcending the medium he was born to.
He was born to love with and be loved in

that body, but his body wanted better for him
and so it helped him change to another body,
one that could turn and face his lover, spread for his lover
thighs like heron wings
and never say sorry. Sorry I've talked so long
about my uncle Rishi, but this isn't something
we talk about in our family. In our family,
it's a pity he never found a wife
beautiful enough to be worthy of his beauty
before he died of an old man's disease, kidney failure,
at the age I am now. Now
I should go write something else, in a different form,
like an essay on karma and rebirth,
or an animal fable, or a sonnet I'll rewrite
as four tercets and a couplet so no one
can tell. Tell no one what I said here,
how I dared betray the way my uncle Rishi
made hoofs of his fists and knees before he died,
made his gullet swallow the enormous fish,
made wings of shoulderblades and flew home,
his untold body changed to other forms.

The lost end up in love with loss.
I'm not my pain. I'm what my pain
became. I am myself because
all those who lose possess their loss,
and all my losses (I've got lots)
taught me the letters of my name.
Love to the end. Nothing is lost.
Possession's afterlife is pain.

Elegy with van Gogh's Ear

Van Gogh rattled his straight razor
in a basin full of water
and stared into his own eyes.
His gray-green irises
began to glow and swirl.
That's when he took off running.
The pain that flamed through him
was flaming through the olive trees,
the whole landscape one forest fire
but everybody picnicking as usual.
He wrapped his ear in newspaper
like roasted peanuts fresh from the stall
and gave it to a woman at the Arles
brothel. Not a whore,
a maid named Gabrielle
who mopped the vomit, gathered bottles,
lifted the sacramental wafer
of a stiff kerchief off the floor.
She worked as a maid in the brothel
because she could not find employment
as a whore. A dog had mauled her
arms and chest too much for that.
They kept her from the clientele
at night because the drunks who saw her
fell silent and set down their glasses.
She had evaded rabies that savage June
but not July's medical bills.
A white dog half her size had knocked her
body to the street and jerked atop her
like an epileptic rapist
until somebody shot it through the head.
The gunshot left her deaf in both ears.

The artist sought her out
that cold December night and gave her
this gift, this fresh and full-grown ear
so she could hear the church bells welcome Christmas
to Arles. You were mangled,
and I am mangled, too, he longed
to say. You paint this brothel
clean again with soap and water,
I scrub the filth off God with brushes.
Her visitor ran off before
she could unwrap the present
dripping on her snowy threshold.
He could not hear her scream
since he was running to a church
at an Auvers of his imagination
where all the windows held the same blue
as the sky behind them. Even
after her police report,
the orphaned ear was left with her.
She buried it behind the brothel,
where clients sometimes staggered out, and unzipped,
and watered it. In time it grew
into a flowering tree that flowered ears
the bees found sweet, Arlesian honey
a deeper amber with a hint of rust.
Gabrielle was still a maid by then,
still paying off the interest on her debt.
Scar tissue glistened on her arms and nipple craters.
One summer night, the stars began
to chase each other clockwise,
and when she touched the flame atop her candle
she came away with her thumb smudged.
She tiptoed to the tree of ears
and whispered into one of them
the thing she wanted most.

The next day, a little after noon,
the whores woke up and found her
naked at the foot of the tree, her body
nineteen years old again and whole
and very cold, as cold as that December
night the artist tried restoring her.
Whines went up from all the stray dogs in Arles.
The girls admired her and stroked her curls.

The Syndrome

Loss of position sense on summer evenings,
The finger pads becoming fireflies
That brighten as they rise. Ability
To manage money seriously impaired.
Angry nostalgia over bygone aesthetics,
Girlfriends, bookstores, religious certainties.
Exaggerated fear of losing son
On summer evenings cupping fireflies
Bewildered in close quarters by their own light.
Loss of the sense of time when lost in words
Experienced as intensely as sensations
And more intensely than the times. Twilight
Detected in the irises. Perceived
Decrease in ease of run compared to last time.
Loss of wanderlust but not of lust.
Rational fear of losing parent, worsened
By habit of subtracting parent's age
From average human life expectancy,
Even while watching parent blow out candles.
Mechanical progression into future
Sleepwalking backwards on a squeaky treadmill.
Loss of the poem on a summer evening
As fingers, lit up, litter laptop keys
With the yellow embers of smashed fireflies.
Newfound lost feeling. Numbness of the tongue.
Persistence, in a dark wood, of the hunt.

Rate Your Pain

after Don Paterson

1) Fleeting prickles, often on the nape of the neck. Can be confused with embarrassment. Vanishes suspiciously within seconds of swallowing baby aspirin.

2) Low-amplitude throb. Benefits from massage with opposite hand. Temporarily forgotten using green tea or online thinkpiece. Vanishes after baby aspirin has had time to digest. Retrospective skepticism regarding its ever being felt.

3) Sharp, but only in certain easily avoided positions. Unexpected recurrence during afternoon racquetball game. Controlled with over-the-counter nonsteroidals already in medicine cabinet but close to expiration. First passing reference in conversation with spouse.

4) Stabbing. Opaque relationship to position or diet. Merits alternation of Tylenol and Aleve. Interferes with meals but not with sex. Canvassing of coworkers regarding home remedies. Irritation with children. First appointment with physician.

5) Constant and radiating. First beads of sweat on brow. Uneasy shifting in seat on subway or bus. Googling of detailed description followed by transient freakout. Careful avoidance of exacerbating positions during sex. Persists in spite of over-the-counter pill cocktails and electric heating pad.

6) Knifelike and unremitting. First drips of sweat off earlobes and tip of nose. Opioid prescription filled. Scanning of online chatrooms for kindred sufferers. Impotence scare. Advice from spouse regarding benefits of yoga.

7) Still knifelike but a bigger knife. Overpriced acupuncture session with relief lasting half the drive home. Online investigation of cupping. Second medical

opinion. Small but significant errors at work caught by discreet colleagues. Stop signs ignored in a state of distraction, but without incident.

8) Machetes lodged in several viscera. Bedsheets soaked. Triple dose of opioid just to see. Leather belt between clenched teeth. Forehead through drywall. Third medical opinion. Striking of youngest child followed by intense remorse.

9) Sulfuric acid in bloodstream. Loss of bowel and bladder control. Blood expressed from tear ducts. Clawmarks across upholstery of minivan driven through closed garage door. Spouse and children sent to stay with in-laws. Normal MRI scan.

10) Natural childbirth through both ear canals. Six remaining opioid pills dissolved into bottle of Stolichnaya. Brown paper bag over shrieking mouth rapidly inflated and crushed. Sheepish phone call to workplace requesting sick day. Nose running constantly with cerebrospinal fluid. Gouging out of eyes with butterknife. Writhing in front yard under flashing blue and red lights. Arms spread out in gratitude for gunshots officers fired as they converge in self-defense.

Autumnal

When he stepped out of the house that morning
to rake the leaves I could have raked,
the screen door clapped home against the house
so hard it echoed. The house was solid because he
was solid. Now the screen swings back and forth
endlessly swishing its net through the air,
more holes than door, like a father
more memories than body. If I step through
that screen door from his absence into his absence,
the other side is the same as this one,
and the only grass that's greener grows
three months behind me. I make the sign
of the cross over my chest to x
myself out. I recheck all the light switches
three times before sleep, touching them
in every room like relics that will heal me.
I knew both grace and predestination once
in my father's voice and my father's hand.
If you're wondering why the voice
doesn't cry in the wilderness anymore,
the leaves have been laid to rest
and the voice laid waste to. These branches
are dreamcatchers, less scaffolding
than space between. Everything passes
through them. Everything passes. Everything is past.

The Turin Horse

When it happened
(we knew for months that it would happen)
I felt, and this is going to seem, I know,
a super highbrow reference, but I felt
like Nietzsche endstage in Turin.
Like I'd just finished up badmouthing
Wagner and Christ and slaves and nice people
and now, while wandering all disheveled
daydreaming dithyrambs and treponemes,
I saw the whipping of the Turin horse.
Somehow the horse was everyone I saw,
and while I didn't throw my arms around them,
I stumbled onward, everywhere about to.
I wanted to explain that yes, my dad
just died, and with him all my high
philosophy. I wasn't up on Sils
Maria anymore. I knew that they
had lost somebody too
they wouldn't talk about, they never talked
about. Don't bother with a brave face, friends!
I'm not an intellectual anymore. I know
the heart, that brown horse, won't move on
no matter how time whips it. I know
your dead and mine are stubborn horses,
and we will throw our arms around them
sobbing with love not at all universal,
what though we tumble through the imago,
our arms enclosing only
the dust motes in a sunlit window floating
in the house where I grew up
the day I have to sell it. My friends,
I was the sole albino pigeon

strutting cooring on the cobblestones
while all of you had bruise-gray feathers
pretending bruised was how you were born.
I'm broken now, like Nietzsche in Turin,
where death is whipping, whipping, whipping
my father stubborn on the cobblestones,
a leather strap between his teeth, his fetlocks
bloody and his round eye darting.
I will not leave I will not leave my boy.
You had this sadness in you all along,
but I believed you frivolous, unphilosophical.
Forgive me, all you secret mourners,
citizens of Turin, believers in the Shroud.
I'm broken, and I need you all to teach me
how not to twitch and rave beneath a shawl
in an asylum for the next eleven years.
I love my slave morality, if that's
what lets me go and hug his suffering.
I'm on the side of all whipped horses now.
I'm in the stables at the birth of tragedy.

The Compass Rose

While those centri-
fugal petals
blossomed in him
for a summer,

we knew up from
down and east from
west, his oeuvre
oriented

like a map to
somewhere better.
We could find out
who we were by

checking with him
for directions.
He could leave us
lost no more than

two magnetic
poles could leave each
other lonely,
or at least we

felt that way. No
more that rose to
navigate our
inland seas, our

endless inlets.
Weather-winded,
winter-withered
windrose, printed

on the flyleaf
of his last book,
tattooed on our
inner wrists—true

north who since has
left us driftwood,
aimless, splintered
in the spindrift.

The Bear

A word peeked sometimes from the cave mouth
only to shuffle back, swallowed, sky-shy,
lost in his memory's russet Lascaux.
The great-granddaughter we set on his lap

played in the far-off, sunlit opening
of a tunnel ninety-one years long,
as noiseless, in spite of the hearing aid,
as a penny striking the floor of a well.

His eyes met ours like a groggy bear's
as he pulled another stone into place
to seal the entrance to himself, to close
the senses that would not close themselves.

When I say my grandfather passed on
last year, what I mean is he passed *inward,*
down the dark slope of a cave, drawn
by the womb rush of a river underground.

The Pediatric Cardiothoracic Surgery Floor

In all the hallways: glossy shots
      and capsule narratives
of Rachel, Kasim, Hailey, Mo,
        the ones who got to live.

They never put up posters, do they,
      of the ones they couldn't save?
Naomi, Hunter, Mickey, Julie,
        whose hearts were just as "brave"

until a seismographic
      zigzag ECG
buckled the rib cage, tumbled the heart
        headlong into the sea,

a dozen whitecoats clustered bedside
      or trooping up the stairs,
the mother sobbing on her phone
        assured and ushered clear

while a panicked student, or panicked intern,
      two fingertips on Kyle's chest
compressed, compressed, compressed, compressed,
        compressed, compressed, compressed

Altarpiece

I flash back to you sometimes
in your bassinet,
your diaper and knit cap,
your loincloth and thorn crown.
Breastbone split with a chisel,
your heart's hinge
is a teak diptych,
the altarpiece of my conversion
into father.

You bore the needlestick
stigmata
on the backs of your hands,
and later, when the veins blew,
on the backs of your feet.
A chest tube scar
still marks
the puncture of that lance
as though a stone from heaven scored you
with its atmospheric
entry-flare.
Through that hole, your soul
burrowed back inside
to nest, as I had prayed,
for good.

They clipped the armboards to the OR table,
prepared you for the sacrificial knife.
Afterward, for three days,
you vanished in a cave of Ativan.

But then you came back to us!
I marveled at the mystery.

All those summers counting euros,
a seeker with a backpack
sunscreened and footsore
from the walking tour,
I used to eye with infidel remove
the gory glories of medieval art.

Midway through my middle age,
I was granted through your grace
transubstantiation
into manhood, understanding
for the first time

Imago Pietatis,
the image of pity

for the son
whose suffering's the one
thing holier than joy.

I can see him at last, the Man of Sorrows,
and glory in his heartsblood.

Boy of Sorrows,
welcome home.

His Vision

I never saw the root of the real
In arboreal flare,
Nor witnessed this man walk on water,
Nor that one float in air.

I sat beneath the bodhi tree;
I felt my body itch.
Between the true cup and the false
I knew not which was which.

My eyes have never blown like fuses
Sparked black upon a wall,
No surge of sight or insight mine,
No whisper, and no call.

My thousand suns have been my twins,
My Beatrice, my wife,
My way to immortality
The living of the life—

No visage singed into a shroud
Or knotted in a tree.
A newborn in a swaddling-cloth
Was the vision given me:

Someday the faces round my sickbed
Will blur and superimpose
Into that single human Face
The visionaries know,

My humble human loves collected
And, for the first time, seen
Intensely, their diffraction
Narrowed to a beam.

The Weaver's Song

I wove myself a boy of wicker.
Daddy, teach me what to fear.
Matches, ants, and the flail of the rain,
But not while Daddy's here.

My kindergarten kindling boy,
My whistle at the marrow.
My rustle, my husk, my huggable scarecrow
Who couldn't spook a sparrow.

I gave him a coat and acorn eyes.
I set him in a chair.
Daddy, patch my wicker elbow
And comb my wicker hair.

Who coaxed him off my porch? The wind,
Gray-haired and stooped and kind.
I should have heard the leaves on the street,
The shudder of the chimes.

The Potter's Field

Something lumpen, something slapped
Wet on a wheel, cupped and spun,
Sculpted; something hollowed, bellied,
Shapely; something held, watered,
Coaxed into a poised amphora.

Soiled hands smooth their own prints
Like still winds pressed to the spinning earth.
Brittle even after the fire,
The vessel is what it holds:
Ashes, ouzo, roses, olive oil.

I never understood your choice,
Or what that haggard savior held
For you, until you told me the part
Of the cemetery where the dirt poor
Returned their poverty to the dirt,

Repossessed, anonymous,
No grave-goods but a prayer,
Used to be called the potter's field—
Barren furrows, fruitful now with clay
Scooped and pulsing in your hand.

Theory of Incompleteness

This Rodinesque
chipped-away-at
demiembodiedness.

What is yet to come into
its sweetness
still green on the stem.

Between two ahems,
this attempt
at a hymn.

Our typically skeptical
head-tilt
when faced with too much neatness.

Our feel for a whole
augmented
by its missing fragments.

These scars and hickeys
rebuffing
spit and polish.

After the fisticuffs
we've only the mistiest memory of,
this gap-toothed grin.

A magnum opus
guessed together
from the notebooks.

Our cosmos, all these
aeons into things,
still forming.

This body we bury
a spore of glory
briefly dormant.

Detachment

They had their hack for suffering, the old
yogis. Even a two-inch levitation
changes the lay of shadows. Better than
the Bo tree's shade is in the Bo tree's branches,
your monkey-mind undressing a banana
while Dobermans bark up at you in vain.
Detachment gets you high, above all pain.
You're parasailing miles above a lake
of fire, sawing sobbing through the cable
until you gust free in a falling flying
quest for a further shore. Detachment puts you
in low earth orbit, lens against the porthole
to photograph your suffering down there—
that Ganges with the lights along it, holy
cities feeding off it like electric
mosquitoes plugged in the mother aorta.
The illness, the love, the illumination
volt back into the flow. You see them brighten
all your suffering from source to delta
until its faultline-fateline blazes white
to match the zigzag of the clear sky's lightning
that struck you years ago, first grief, first gift.
Keep going, higher. Gravity and you
uncouple. Atoms start to break their bonds,
like oxygen's with hydrogen: Those tears
you're crying aren't water anymore.
The synapse where your pain was crossing widens.
Your neurotransmitters are spilling free
and sprinkling space, which doesn't feel a thing.
Neither do you, because you have dissolved,
at one with everything at last. Nirvana.

I'm not all one. There is no one
me—I alone am many I's.
Their once-upon-a-times become
the now I am. There is no want
of others in me, their ego sum
the zero sum behind my eyes.
In one me, there's an everyone,
and here, in everyone, am I.

Letters to Myself in My Next Incarnation

Hello again from who you were
Before. Hello before to who
I'll be again. I think we both knew
This was going to be awkward,
And not just grammatically.
I wanted to write you a note
To familiarize you
With the controls,
But the body is a vehicle
The soul relearns
How to drive by crashing
Into other bodies.
This is what they call wisdom,
And by "they," I mean fools
Like us, and by "wisdom"
I mean, like Plato,
Memory. What I love here,
Poems and women mostly,
I know you can't remember,
But they were worthy of my love
Because they fooled me into wisdom
Using pleasure.
If you are reading this
I am already
Dead. If you are reading
This I am already
Living. Stranger, I
Have no advice for you.
I only wrote this
Because I was lonely
And wanted someone
To talk to,

Even if it was only
Myself. Why do we
Write anything
If not to pass along a valediction
From the echo
Whose echo we are,
If not to say
To the echo
We expect to become
Hello
Hello
Hello

•

Motherless infinituplets
Separated
By birth

At the end of every flatline
You and I
Arrive in rhyme

Words to a Requiem
Our choir of one
Must sing

We embryos in amber strung
On a single
Umbilical string

•

Sift the chaff of faces, voices, friendships
Until you find her. Dancing with that woman

Was the only reason
Tripwire desire didn't get me this time.
Duplicate, dupe, I know you well enough
And hope this poem finds you early,
So I can tell you: *Kid, be patient! Slow down!*
She's looking for you too
Right now, she's busy
Waving off the moths
Hot for her incandescence! All those boys
Are just the background noise
She listens past to hear
Your past and hers, harmonic in the moment . . .
So patience, patience, stop yourself
From taking what's on offer
In the future where you're lost to me
But never will be lost to her, a future
That, like my present, I imagine,
Has everything on offer cheap and fast.
Slow down. You'll recognize her, trust me,
Even if it isn't right away.
I recognized her after eighteen years.
In this life, I've got pictures of us
On a lawn in Dover, Ohio,
Playing as toddlers, playing toddlers
When really we were braided ancients, sampling
Parallel play, sampling
Crushes on each other, sampling friendship
Until the air began to torque between us,
Full-blown tornado of remembered love
Snapping us free of childhood
To spiral us skyward in a single cord,
Umbilical and nourishing a single future
That she will cradle one day in a hospital gown,
Exhausted after giving birth,
Your arm in turn around her shoulder:

Three bodies, father, mother, newborn
Nestling one inside the other,
My past and all the pasts before mine, too,
Inside your musically patterned present
Nested, life in life in life.

•

It's cold out there,
A real blizzard,
So I am pouring in this thermos for you
The memory you cannot do without.
Remember when the love transitioned: when
She took my heat and sweat into the shower
And didn't close the bathroom door behind her.
I waited, then went in to watch her
Seven veiled in shower steam
Turning beneath the water, turning
To find me watching her. She didn't startle.
Her finger traced a heart
In the condensation on the shower glass.
I'm trying, self, to love her selflessly
So I can pass her on to you because
The one thing better than the memory
Of this love has to be reliving this love,
Your years together interlocking
Like zipper teeth toward your chin,
The parka zipped at last, the heat locked in
As you force the door, and brace for the blast,
And turn your face into the winter wind,
This thermos glowing, sheltered in your hands,
And snow aswirl where I used to stand.

•

Beyond the Kuiper belt,
at the behest of some
circadian imperative,
souls fluster as one
off a lake of frozen mercury
and swirl back to this world,
buoyed on each other's wake.

They have the earth imprinted
deeper than a memory.
Monarch butterflies
come winter can
remember oyamels
they've never settled on
deep in a Mexico
they've never visited.

The dead are one aurora
incorporealis
shuttling between a north
of water clocks, a south
of water steaming away, a north
of sundials, a south
of hydrogen fusion.

In Norway, near the equinox,
the best time and place to watch
the transmigratory pattern
of souls across the night sky,
my soul will kick the luminescence
off its legs like a rescue
diver shedding his jeans.

I will seek my next parents
among the battle dead,
the glorious, the wrung sponges
of young couples cooling
in each other's sweat.
I want a father dreaming
of firecracker chrysanthemums
a blue furlong beyond his boyhood.
I want a mother dreaming
of a goddess on a tiger.

Part of this is instinct
and part of it delight:
Stranger, signal me
from way on down the tracks.
Wave me in with orange wands
because I have been flying
an eternity to land in time
at last and grow the hands
I need to feel your face.

•

The peak that paints the lake
is quick to break.

A height becomes a depth,
a life a death.

An Eiger sinks beneath
the eager cleat

as seeking shows us what
we sought is not.

To find a seeker's pleasure
in self-erasure

the mountaineer must wish
herself to mist.

•

My body is a pawprint in the snow,
My memory, a snowman in the spring,
A little time, and then it's time to go,

So sing, my momentary Snowman, sing
The song that goes like O and o and o,
For shape is brief, and time is everything,

And everything is melting into flow,
Where graveyards, gone to gray, must go to green
Again, and all the memories regrow,

For shape imprints, implies a life unseen,
A charm against the cold, the pock of paws
Continuing as footprints through the scene,

Where children stack a snowman in the thaw
And sing to springtime O and o and o,
The shape of time, the letter of the law,

The song I shape from memories of snow.

•

When I recollect
In the still of your quickening,
I will condense, remade
In an underwater image
Truer maybe to myself
Than I have been in this life.

I have lived out my life
Seeking a self
In no one else's image.
By the time you read me,
I'll have felt your quickening,
Fetal, fatal. Collect

My words and reconnect
With me where I quicken in
Your wrists. I have remade
My reflection in your image.
You're how I reimagined myself.
Stranger, outlive my life.

•

Foundling on the temple steps
With all your birth tokens
Stolen,

Impossible
Walking dossier, your face
A rogue's gallery,

Your passport
A palimpsest
Of noms de plume,

My future homonym,
My future human
Meme, my futile name's

Skull-shucked
Plucked-spleen picked-clean
Mummified remains,

Loose translation of a gospel
Apocryphal
To begin with,

Prehistoric daddy longlegs
Hatching
From an amber egg,

Segue
Between myself
And myself,

Why do
I pile up these metaphors
For you

When a metaphor
Is all you'll ever be
Of me?

•

I didn't pick my parents,
But I am picking yours.
With all I do,
I save up for a berth, for passage

First class west to the New World
Where a house is waiting for you.
Two balloons
Are knotted to the mailbox,
Now a little loose
And bouncing in the breeze.
Both parents, all four grandparents—
They're recording your arrival
On their phones.
Love, safety, self-discipline,
Prosperity, good books, good genes:
I wish you
All the bourgeois, suburban blessings
I've wished my kids
Because I'm parenting
A fate, I'm narrowing a list
Of childhoods
Like kindergartens
To send you to.
I didn't used to be a decent man,
But fatherhood improved me.
When I was younger, kid,
I spiked the karmic punch,
And now what's in me
Is bound to be in you.
But don't you worry,
I'll be good for you from now on.
You, my spirit changeling.
Metamorphic orphan.
Only child.

Two dark points make the den of seeing.
Me, I want to be all eyes,
a vanishing point to canvass being,
perspectives drawn into my seeing.
If my one I can make a we, then
two black holes beyond the ken of seeing
will make my eye, through art, all eyes.

Resurrection: His Hands

First thing he did was clap his hands
against his eyes, as if he'd gouged
them out with hairpins. Only this
was someone else's son, and sin.
The hands appeared to blink.
He looked out through his peephole
stigmata, stereoscopic fisheyes
set in the locked door of the kingdom,
and there he saw a million strangers
in the hotel hallway waiting
to be let in. As he studied
each face, inventing names for them,
a fire broke out on the ground floor,
or maybe it was always burning,
the whole hotel—its pool, its fire
escapes, its continental breakfast,
bread basket full of bleached white stones.
The screams, the faces warping, fists
pounding the door made both the door
and his own risen body shudder.
He staggered back from the burning mob
packed in the hall like cattle cars,
hands dropping so fast they gave
a little whistle as the air went through,
a whistle heard by none but dogs,
all the stray mutts in Jerusalem
rushing to lick his holey hands,
mad for the smell of meat on the wind.

Virus

Neither video
Nor bacterium,

Doorknob-slobber droplet-
Borne mysterium,

Born of nothing, knowing
Only how to breed

Like some dandelion-clock-less
Dandelion seed,

Protean protein,
Hijacker, safe-cracker,

Magical papyrus-
Scrap of genome

Sealed with a cork
To sail the maelstrom,

Mimetic malice,
Code and chalice,

Yours the message
All the Muses sing:

*Purity of heart
Is to will one thing*

Tripping on Metaphors

A line is spider
silk cross-linking
an inkling with

another of
its ilk. A line is
a tripwire that

when tripped on
closes a neural
circuit. What detonates

is a significance
that trips
up logic since

metaphor
is to logic
what analogy is

to twins, what psilocybin
is to water
from the faucet

because it
hallucinates
a kinship of some kind,

some never-before-
seen symmetrical
design of being

                between
this love and that fire,
            that dagger and this stare,

this night
            and that mare. If light
is a metaphor

            for truth,
a metaphor
            takes a leap of faith

on a dare.
            We must take care
to trip on every

            metaphor's
nonlinearity
            of line.

Falling is
            the metaphor that
sends us flying.

Rigidity

The spider
knows the window
  screen he picks

his way
  across is nowhere
he could live.

  These cables
(clearly strung
  by someone

extraordinarily
  able) hold
no hunger,

  no tremble,
no spit,
  no give.

No gnat
  or midge, though
sure to

  stop
short at this
  grid, would ever

feel that sticky
  bouncy
webbiness

             that gets
the killing
             done.

The legs that climb
             these lines
divine

             how a brilliant
& distant
             & orderly

mind, by falling
             head over
spinnerets

             in love
with spinning,
             totally

forgot
             why webs
are spun.

Ode to a Jellyfish

Ghost truffle
unruffled
by rough weather,

electrically
whiskered
saltwater whisper,

colorless and odorless,
tangible patch
of poison gas

inhaling, exhaling,
all skirt and no legs,
parasailing

on sigh after sigh
of inner under-
water wind,

your sentient
tentacles
cobweb-thin

serenely
kissing fire
up my daughter's shin

Observing Orpheus

I hear the meaning turn back in his throat
like Eurydice on the way up from the darkness.
Music's meaning is its making. As for me,
I am one more animal in his entourage,
learning a new thirst, finding a new south.
None of us knew we had this instinct in us.
If deserts hide wildflowers until first rain,
bright ears are blossoming out of our skulls.
He doesn't have much longer. I know this myth.
A God douses the fire with a beehive.
The Maenads smear their faces with a warpaint
made of stoneground fireflies and pine sap.
Hands—hands like his, that drew music
through lyre strings into our forest
like pieces of bread through a prison fence—
are reaching for his body now, his lyre.
Their weapons are hands, nothing but hands.
They are infinite. They are enough.

Four Ways of Looking at Argus

1. *His Vigil*

These hundred eyes, these hundred balloons
Tied to the boy-small wrist of my mind
Are down to ninety-nine.
I lost one to a beesting late last June—
I never thought of them as fragile
Until that pinprick broke my vigil.
I'm slowing down. I didn't blink in time.

I have no inkling why I keep
This vigil—surely not to watch,
Panoptic from this mountaintop,
A heifer drifting off to sleep?

I'm here, I must be here, to see
A signal fire from the east
That warns of Olympus under siege
And Ares gory from a rout,
Athena's owl's eyes gouged out,
The naiads naked in a pen,
The whole world given up to men.

The Gods will need a monster then.

2. *After Martial*

Hermes was in a fix: He needed lullabies
        To shutter Argus's one hundred eyes
And get the tethered heifer—coal-eyed Io—free
        Of Hera's peacock-panoptic olive-tree.

He sang the songs his mother Maia sang to him,
>But five eyes flicked awake when one eye dimmed.

So Hermes ventured lines of poetry, and all
>Those hundred eyes began to roll and loll,

Miraculously shut with hexametric verse.
>I trust that story, Zoilus—I've heard *yours*.

3. *Visual Field*

. . . Argus started out as a cyclops, she said as she moved on to the next slide, but that one cycloptic eye divided and subdivided out of control, mitotically overeager, cancerous, until a heavy headdress of one hundred eyeballs made his shoulders stoop, an enormous clump of frog eggs, each one yolked with an iris. Now if two eyes provide us with depth perception, imagine the effect of one hundred. How deeply Argus must have seen, chronologically and subatomically, the surfaces of things to come all velvety with quarks! Once you see this, or should I say *visualize* this through Argus's eyes, you'll see how Argus, guarding Io, was in fact in a state of acute torment, forced to focus on a single transient creature in the near field while his vision ranged naturally over light years and frames of reference. Imagine the strain of being forced to look at the tip of your own nose for months on end. In all likelihood, Argus saw far in advance the scheme of Hermes, who meant to lull him to sleep and brain him and abscond with Io, but Argus allowed the trick to be played on him, grateful for the mercurial music and words that eased all his eyes so mercifully to sleep, and granted him, at long last, the bliss of not seeing . . .

4. *His Anatomy*

His hundred eyes were never spread
In a peacock fan across his head—
Just two up top, like yours or mine.
Each eye, though, nested forty-nine,
An egg no Fabergé designed,
Their pupils perfectly aligned
So that one beam could thread them all—

A needle sung through corneal cauls—
And crackle up the optic nerve.
Each eye observed itself observe,
A metaphysiology of sight
That so interiorized insight
Argus could see a given scene
As picture-in-picture, mise en abyme.
So much awareness in one being
Made him essentially All-Seeing.
That's why the God of thieves disguised
Himself and deviously devised
A trick to thwart those eyes in eyes
In eyes in eyes in eyes in eyes,
Decentered, sleepy, floating free,
Ball-compasses bumped, off by degrees.
His gaze grew hazy, lazy-eyed,
His fine-tuned spheres askew inside.
The trickster's quicksilver pocketknife
Filled the night watchman up with night.
His eyes shocked wide, like mouths left gaping,
Never saw the thief escaping,
Or darkness tiptoeing away,
Or daylight shaking him awake.

Visionary Sonzal

Keen eyes read the top row, staring straight ahead until the words unfocus.
G, then something, then D. . . . If only that middle letter were in focus!

On this eye chart, every focal point is a vanishing point.
Desire dilates pupils. We can't keep the world in focus.

Did you see your blinded savior when he stood here bleeding?
Or did the half light from his sockets blur your focus?

Glassy-eyed architect, you've pored over the heavens long enough.
What's pouring over us is rain. Train your eyes on earth now. Focus.

        Some eyes see the world as it one day might be.
            It is the compassionate who look away.

        Unless art is a glass of acid flung at downcast reading eyes.
          The most God-focused people are the last to look away.

        The world's a Magic Eye illusion. Focus beyond the surface,
          And the suffering emerges. Amit, why do you look away?

Neuroastrogenesis

A migraine heats the wires red behind
the panel   seizures down a power line
& slap it writhing   writing   on the pavement
the problem with a problem of the brain is
you never cure it   only manage it
the fuses thumbed across again   the bucket
ascending from the truck   to hitch things up
until the next storm messes with the grid
a *tumor* means a *swelling*   what swells here
is starstuff   layer by chatoyant layer
until whatever sand grain got inside
the cloister   has become a pearl that
backlights the eardrum's opal shaving
ossicles ashiver   eavesdropping on light

There's no electroshock   no once-a-day
to manage neuroastrogenesis
no burrhole in the skull   to cut you clean
& plunk that fireball into a basin
no triggers to avoid   & no vaccine

I got my diagnosis   at thirteen

Some people   said my doctor   studying
my EEG like a zagging seismograph
demanding mass evacuations   some
unlucky people   grow a star inside
their brains   that's not a bad thing in itself
the problem is   not every womb is hooked up
to a birth canal   the brain is like that
she said   it has its ovaries   its tubes
its uterus   but things conceived inside it

have no way of getting out   & so
they grow   the skull is bone   it can't expand
you see the risk of all that pent-up heat
developing a heart   & growing feet

My parents drove me home   I took
my two proverbial aspirin   & melted
letters off a page by staring at them
I felt the words begin to orbit me
like orphanyms   they tugged my empty pockets
begging meaning   when my mother gave me
Ayurvedic remedies   I spooned
my turmeric   & told her it was helping
but she could see my pupils for herself
surprised like cat eyes creeping past a flashlight

If I don't die of it   I'll live with it
even this knot   of fusing hydrogen
lodged in the crook   of my corpus callosum
If I don't die of it   I'll birth my star
Alpha Centauri   unreachably
far off   blowtorching its way out   dead center
through my forehead   first a dot   & then
a lashless fissure   splitting with a hiss
my third eye bulging   pulsing   alien
fixing on the sun   to find out who blinks first

The Irreversible Spread of the Gypsy Moth

The only source of new light
in the cosmos is the dreaming
gypsy moth. They live just
seven days, long enough
to make a heaven and an earth
and chew down North America's
last balsam firs. I take comfort
in the thought that species
other than my own
are spraying their napalm
genomes across the landscape.
I know my species well
enough. Virality's
the only virtue
we revere. I'd love this flake
of earthly dandruff,
noiseless, unassuming,
to beat us at what we do best.
I wouldn't mind it if
the gypsy moth inherits
the air that we denature,
and under the sign
of the Romà at that—
our scuffed nomadic no ones,
their apartness so pervasively
a part of them
they never soiled exile
by dreaming up a homeland.
The loudest colors, splashed
together, lose themselves in brown,
the moth-mute brown
that daydreams daylight for us.

Even better is their Latin
name: *Lymantria dispar,*
Destroyer of the inequality.
Either everything one shining now
or everything one dark.

We're not the past. We're what the past
became. But we remember who
we are and build ourselves to last
by never treating pasts as passed.
Stock tickers, towers, laptops crash,
and all our tick tock starts anew.
Now that the past is not the past,
who can remember what to do?

Reverse Colonization

1. *Kipling Sonzal*

When my father was young, *center* meant *west*.
Crowded off the edge of home, he went west.

People, like heliotropes, follow the gold.
In those days, the brightest sons were sent west.

Love for a son they'd yet to hold
Beckoned my bookish parents west.

In that new world, the boy's dreams were old.
He found himself born to wealth in a spent west.

> Quicksilver slivers globe and glint.
> Drop me, and drops of me flow east.

> Where I intend to end
> There is no west, no east.

> "All these comforts, Amit, and you're still a malcontent?
> There's nothing for you here. Go east, young man, go east."

2. *Hive Mind Sonzal*

Darkness has descended on Europe, and I am lightly buzzed.
The drug we're doing goes by the street name *ishq*. Don't fight the buzz.

Religion's a buzzkill, but to each his own fix.
Our Father, we ask of you this day our nightly buzz.

Pass out on the mosque steps, and you can expect a few kicks.
That's what happens when the rightly guided meet the rightly buzzed.

Simply add refrain to rhyme, and mix.
This cocktail got the Sufis mighty buzzed.

Great Pan is dead, but I find his flute fallen in the reeds.
I've just licked my lips when out of a stop there crawls a wasp.

I bite her, but never hard enough she bleeds
For fear her pheromone red will call the wasps.

"One sting, Amit, and your throat swells up, you can't breathe.
Why does God make you pray beneath that shawl of wasps?"

3. *Etymology of Wog*

Worthy Oriental Gentleman, he said, was really just a back-formation from
the word, obviously tongue-in-cheek—the real origin was polliwog, that is,
tadpole, that is, they were calling our forefathers armless legless helpless slips
atwitch in a swarthy Oriental backwater, but the good thing about us, a race of
polliwogs on polliwogs begotten, was when we came of age we could handle
the shore and the shallows alike, culturally amphibian, inflating our throats
and tattooing continents on the rounded stretched skin and inflating our
throats even more until we floated birthday-balloon-like off the muck into our
third and unexpectedly quite native element, the air

4. *Immigration Ghazal*

Geography is fate. English reads from west to east.
Fate is calligraphy. Arabic writes from east to west.

One of two elsewheres always tugged and teased the west:
For her finest, the heavens; for the rest, the east.

The sailors had red beards, bad teeth, and wheezing chests. The east,
Assumed the grand vizier, would be the one that seized the west.

Smallpox and Christ were fleas on this angelic beast, the west.
A savage salvation blasted, blinded, blessed the east.

I knew how western money dispossessed the east
But eagerly contracted what diseased the west.

The blood in my veins, the vaccines in my blood: My east, my west
So confluent they've made my east my west, my west my east.

5. Ancient Regime Ghazal

It's spring in the labyrinth, but we waste it looking for a thread out.
We realize Eden is Eden only after we have to get out.

Strange how the world keeps the shape of a beach ball
Though all its breath and color have been let out.

Were things ever really that good, or were they just
Never this bad? We use silk scarves to hide slit throats.

No novus ordo seclorum. No New World.
No way to set things right. No way to set out.

Nostalgia? For *what*? Strange, how in my nonwhite heart
Faith in the Western World defends its last redoubt.

6. The Colony

What looked like a scaleable low mountain, she said, perfect for goring with a
flag or surveying the native infantry's encampments, proved to be an anthill,
of an as-yet-undocumented species, not the black ant, not the red ant, but
the brown Deccan ant impossibly prolific and dangerous to disturb: The first

explorer to set foot on that mountain found his body changing color in agony as the mountain encroached along his body, grains of dirt sprouting legs and stingers and charging over his knees, his crotch, his navel, his neck, until he turned to his coolies and cried *Bachao, bachao,* which means *Save me, save me,* this saving being what the missionaries who arrived with him had promised to do for the coolies: the same coolies who, born the color of those ants, turned away and began dividing the sahib's supplies and equipment among themselves, fairly and quietly, making sure to toss an offering of toffee to the ants, who melted it into their busy mass, where the sahib's torso and pith helmet retained only approximate contours, like some hominid fossil from before recorded history trampled faceless by generations of rain

7. *Sojourn in the Bungalow*

in memory of V. S. Naipaul

Call Subbarao here. I want you all to see something. To have some idea. Subbarao!

Yes Colonel sahib.

Tell our visitor who you are.

The dust of Colonel sahib's feet, Colonel sahib.

What did you eat with, before I found you?

My fingers.

What did you read with, before I found you?

I did not read.

What do you read now, Subbarao?

Ji sahib, biographies of Plutarch, sir.

Whom do you like?

Ji—Alcibiades, sahib.

Who is better than Alcibiades? Who is the father and grandfather and great-grandfather of Alcibiades?

You, Colonel sahib.

You like Alcibiades. How do you feel about me?

I love you.

For when your own priests knocked you about and spat on you, I picked you up and dusted you off.

That is why I love you, sahib.

And what do I hit you with, Subbarao, when you displease me?

The flat of your hand, like a husband. The sole of your sandal, like a gentleman.

And how do you feel about me when I hit you, Subbarao?

I hate you, Colonel sahib.

And you will rise against me, you dog? Quote Plutarch at me? Brutus. And do what else?

Worship your feet, sahib. Pour dust on my head and cry.

You will go back to your village in shame. What will you do on the roadside?

Squat to pass foul matter, sahib.

And when I drive past you?

I will chase after the auto.

Begging, with your hand drifting up to your mouth and back down again, over and over, your head nodding in plaintive figure-eights.

Yes sahib, begging for the light of your eyes, sahib.

And why?

Because I love you.

You hate me.

I love you.

Casus Belli

Words have
atmospheres,
  and atmospheres

  cause interference.
The more
  revelatory

  distortions happen
just below our
  hearing, where

  a war
of words can
  warp into

  a war of
wars—on the high-
  horse-crowded

  road to which our
one true Gods are one
  more goad.

Deaths of the Eminent Philosophers

This one jumped into Mount Etna,
as free as free will gets.
This one died in his childhood bedroom
crushed by student debt.

This one sought the philosopher's stone
and brained himself when he found it.
This one saw a horse get flogged
and threw his arms around it.

This one died chin-deep in dung,
convinced it would cure his dropsy.
This one overdosed on morphine
in Catalonia fleeing Nazis.

This one died of erysipelas,
a fancy skin disease
that sounds like the name of a soulless sophist
who snitched on Socrates.

This one died of flu, a very
unmemorable death
in a town unforgettably hard to pronounce,
Penrhyndeudraeth.

Death endures the Gifford Lectures.
Death is unimpressed.
Materialists can't make the countdown
matter any less.

In the magical cave whose open-sesame
is Cogito ergo sum,
the crown and the coins, the lamp and the genie
illuminate a tomb.

Descartians, Kantians, Marxists all
arrive at the selfsame crux
as cell by cell the sum of all their
cogitations deconstructs.

Combat

We, the soon to die, salute you. That was what
the gladiators shouted on the way in.
Boar's-head helmets, tridents, broadswords, fishnets—
dressed to kill, they literally killed
each other, or the lions shipped from Barbary
worth more than any human in the show.
"We, the soon to die" takes five words in English,
one for each of the senses. Latin fits it
in one word, *morituri,* which might well
be Japanese for that one blowfish
that either tastes how sex should feel
or kills you. Rome was always dying—
it lived on top of death, the catacombs
a sister city with her own ambitions.
The gladiators knew which Rome all roads
were leading to, the one aboveground or
the one below. They knew that Claudius
or Nero or whatever sucker sat there
was only waiting out the customary
eight months before his bodyguards would bury
their knives in him. But what the lions knew
was something else entirely. Slow and calm,
they licked their paws of the last round's Christians.
The cage door rattled skyward. Free of tension
about the future, free of the future tense,
subject to death but never in its power,
they strolled toward the sunlight on the blades.

The Plague Comes to Bologna

The humanists are dying,
Bubonic inkwells in their groins
Lanced with a neoclassic quill
Eliciting Latinate groans.

After the rotten-truffle sweat smell
Gives way to the death smell,
An undertaker with an oxcart
Nods at the friar for the death knell.

The humanists are dying
Like so many staggered bees
Of some selective, secretive disease
Collapsing all their colonies.

The butcher and the cobbler just don't care.
And neither does the mayor.
The undertaker cares
If he'll be climbing stairs.

The humanists are dying out
As each one gets what he deserves
For doing Ciceronian rewrites when
The Lord desired him to serve.

Into the fire with his clothes and bedpan,
His wooden spoon, his reading stand,
And on the desk, in the living light,
The pages in his sloping hand.

Kicking the Can Down the Road

You've been walking
backwards
for so long

it doesn't feel
so awkward
anymore.

In fact, it has
become the norm
to claim your side

just scored. The goal
has always been
to pass along

the road from
Washington
to nowhere

this can that's
taken on
the contour

of an intricately
dinted, infinitely
polyhedral

soccer ball.
You're hoping
there's some road

to go yet
so that when it's
        your turn

you won't turn
        to find a wall,
given that all

        the experts
you have heard
        have warned

that the can,
        once opened,
is sure to air

        a generation's
worth of
        worms

and that whoever
        opens it
will be the one

        who has to blink
into the light
        and squirm.

The Smithsonian Museum of Supernatural History

"To your left, you will see what appear to be nuggets of charcoal,
but in fact, they're considerably rarer than lunar rocks.
This glass case is airtight and soundproof. Contain them
in anything less, and the screams in these hell stones (think
of the waves in a conch shell you hold to your ear)
would echo throughout the exhibit, if not the museum.
At noon, we'll be feeding the hell stones. You heard me:
They need us to feed them. Now, what does a hell stone eat?
They prefer those parts of the body that grow after death.
So fingernails, mostly, that sizzle on contact and vanish.
Our docents, trimming their mustaches, gather the trimmings
in Ziplocs and sprinkle them over the stones like fish food.
The crackle they make when they eat, I am told, resembles
the neck of a hanged man the moment the trapdoor drops,
though to *my* ear, it's more like Rice Krispies in milk.
There isn't a hell anymore, not as Jonathan Edwards
conceived it. That hell and the furnace in Hansel and Gretel
are equally fairy-tale, equally hokey antiques.
Though some of our curators note that our hell stones still
have an appetite. Some have suggested the screams
I was talking about are a war cry, or mating call.
Just a couple of stones could rebuild the entire inferno.
I guess that we house them the same way the CDC houses
its vials of smallpox and polio. Keeping a sample
of what you eradicate guards you against a recurrence.
It's like that for all our museum exhibits: the trace
of the god in the comic-book hero, the trace of election
in fame. Such a project is, naturally, not without danger.
This glass case? It's bulletproof. Nevertheless, we have had
to replace it twice since the artifacts went on display.
In the dark, after closing, they pelt themselves against it,
a hailstorm that stops at a swing of the night watchman's flashlight."

Apocalypse Shopping List

Lead-lined gonad guards.
>   Lysol (radiation sickness causes *killer* runs).
Breadboxes, to bury stillbirths.
>   Flare guns, glue guns, gun guns.
Marijuana brownies for the burn units.
>   Ersatz shrouds (viz., bedsheets, towels, sails).
Triple-earwig-pincer Biohazard labels.
>   Fun Size Snickers Not Labeled for Individual Sale
But good to barter in a pinch.
>   Amputation pails.
Seeing Eye dogs bunker-kenneled in Kennebunkport, Maine,
>   To jog the flash-blind through uranium rain.
Astronaut ice cream for the bedbound.
>   Catheters (various calibers).
Lice combs to harvest protein.
>   Steri-Strips.
Spike strips.
>   Benadryl, good for baby's colic or mommy's hives.
Teriyaki turkey jerky.
>   Paperback copies of *Slaughterhouse-Five*.
Bullhorns for the water rioters.
>   Fire hoses for the riot police.
Wooden stakes, because you never know.
>   Four-ounce jars of Fleischmann's yeast.
Gallon jugs of Zen.
>   Rabbit traps, for the mice of the future.
Bear traps, for the men.

This is me. I am no other.
Though others see another here,
I didn't write him. They're the author
of that pseudohim, that other
who's no one's son and no one's brother.
Who is that I? It's me, I fear.
From now on, I can be no other
than this unseen one othered here.

Replacement Fertility (I)

Afternoons were lattes and Bolaño
then somehow she was forty-one
and I was tenure-track
but out of love. So what? No one
we knew was having babies
except the friends we didn't *know*
know anymore. I feared
the beard and baby sling. She feared
the lack of time to write, and stretchmarks
Time that spry albino puma
would claw into her flanks,
and what her turning forty-two
did to the likelihood of Trisomy 21.
By then it was too late. By now
it is too late. We wanted
pleasure, and pleasure we took
in big mouthfuls of foam to slake
a thirst we didn't realize
was all along for babies. So we weren't
like two rare albino pumas
scientists around the world
were cheering on in vain. We fucked
like highly educated rabbits careful
not to jeopardize their goals. She popped
sterility with easy daily dosing,
and I pulled out to make extra sure.
We wanted pleasure more
than joy, or any rumored joy
that from our distance seemed a marathon
in cleats with diaper bags on no sleep
toward debt. The thing is, she
was working on that poem

and I was highlighting in my Arendt,
who had no babies,
or was that Simone Weil,
or de Beauvoir, someone
so terminally European
she might have had an interesting baby
but if required to raise it
would have written fewer books
and so been that much less of interest
to her at forty-three
or me a shutting office door
away from middle-aged adultery.
I didn't, by the way. In case you're wondering.
It isn't just the Enfamil and bounce house
that scare the pants back on me.
We didn't. And why would we?
No one we knew was having babies.
Everyone we didn't
was, though. We can smell them
voting in surrounding counties,
wintering in hutches,
storing up their young.
Come morning, we can count
six sets of footprints in the snow.
They must be pacing
out the property for later.
It is only right.

1979

The mob that knifed the sentry knew Hafiz.
The mob had dedicated to Hafiz

A park with pigeons in downtown Tehran
A mere two weeks before it threw Hafiz

Through the glass house of the embassy,
Brickbats of spine and glue that flew Hafiz

Into a future where no books could live
Unless approved as good and true. Hafiz—

Starry-eyed lush with Shiraz on his breath,
The Persian miracle half Rumi's, half his—

Danced with the students on a burning roof,
Clinked toasts with an inkwell in the news office

Because Hafiz was young and knew no better,
Wine condensed on his tongue like dew, Hafiz

Conspiring on the tongues of priests and gunmen
Masked, veiled like the Beloved, who blew Hafiz

Like a kiss at all of us who drink and rhyme,
At all of us who know the true Hafiz

As an ambassador from the hidden kingdom
Where rooftop sniper fire cues Hafiz,

His rhymes, when broadcast by the muezzin,
A rain of red wine out of the blue, Hafiz

Making the revolutionaries dreidel
(Spinning's the best way to pursue Hafiz),

Making Marines cry Allah, mobs cry Oorah,
Lovers who never knew they knew Hafiz.

The Rumi Variations

1.

My mother tongue had a single word for *myself* and *yourself.*
The word for *self* was *God,* so when you said "my God" you meant "your self."

In our Book, she explained, everything means something else.
The words stand for God. The white space represents yourself.

Mahdi, Twelfth Imam, Messiah: smoke rings in a cyclone.
Why show up, they ask, where *you* are barely present yourself?

In this city, everyone's awaiting someone else.
The Immanence commands: *Absent yourself.*

You're always asking us the way to Mecca.
Kafir, maybe it's time you went yourself.

99.

Sing of heaven. You have to open your mouth to kiss that world.
Sing of people. Visionaries look directly at this world.

After a Night Journey to heaven, they come back to this world.
Worldliness can be otherworldly. This world *is* that world.

Evil needs enemies *now.* Seekers of heaven, resist that world—
Heaven's purpose is down here, to serve as a catalyst world.

God's eyes are an atlas of the past, his inner world the saddest world.
We tried to fix America. Who knew how much we'd miss that world?

1001.

Something's been burrowing into my brain. I feel it laying larvae.
Gray matter, white matter, neuron neuron neuron: layered larvae.

My prayers twitch and hatch into limber nymphs,
Still playing the word games they played as larvae.

Under my breath I see God's shadow swim:
A spiny, whiskered fish that preys on larvae.

The old lush took flight. No one imagined wings on *him!*
Just goes to show you, what look like earthworms may be larvae.

When you pray for wings, specify what kind.
A handful of pearls can hatch into mosquitoes.

Doubt is standing water in the mind,
A shallowness that brews mosquitoes.

"Did you trek inland, Amit, and find the divine?
Or were you discouraged by a few mosquitoes?"

∞.

I said the Ninety-Nine Names.
And then, somehow, the rhymes came.

Kafir's mirror image is *rafiq*, is *friend*.
I recite and I scoff in skewed time frames.

Rumi, too, they shut out of the Blue Mosque.
I've found companionship in this sublime shame.

I'm most spontaneous when most in form.
Only a tame mind would find these lines tame.

Amit's meaning, in Hebrew, is *friend*.
I know the name of your God. Can you name mine?

Innocents Abroad

The cathedral-as-
museum: Dinosaur bones,
buried in the air.

"This is our stop. That
English isn't spoken here
goes without saying."

Futures breed like the
rabbits capitalists reach
in their top hats for.

"Of course they hate us!
If you were them, admit it,
wouldn't you hate you?"

Swab your cheek and check
your genetics. We've all got
a touch of Genghis.

"The Saudis wanted
to build it bigger than St.
Paul's, *next* to St. Paul's."

The way they pronounce
"guard" I thought she was saying
changing of the god.

I came here to see
what London looks like. Surprise:
London looks like me.

This, Winston, is how
you conquer a country. Not
with guns. With children.

True Believer

"What men truly want is peace,"
Says the last one true prophet.
Peace feels so like submission
Good prophets can fool most men.
For the rest, there's the hammer,
Followed by a gentle tongue

To sweet-talk the wounds. A tongue
Works wonders keeping the peace,
But wonder-workers keep hammers
Handy. Ask any prophet
Who's spent some time among men:
Supervising submission

Is no humble lamb's mission.
You must learn to scold in tongues.
The cold acumen cold men
Make war with is of a piece
With the poet's and prophet's.
Sometimes words, sometimes hammers,

Sometimes words shaped like hammers
Bring about the submission
So cherished by all prophets,
Heart of gold or golden-tongued.
Submission has a certain poise,
A certain beauty. What men

Want is the same thing women
Want: that is, a sound hammer
Against the skull, and the peace
That sees stars. True submission
Begins in the throat, the tongue.
No God but this. No Prophet

But this. You see the prophet's
Quite wise when it comes to men:
Simple thoughts in a simple tongue,
And, just in case, the hammer.
Some men call peace, submission.
Some men call submission, peace.

The prophet nods and strokes his piece.
His yes men are on a mission.
Stick out your tongue, says the hammer.

Grooming

I shaved my face, and they called me doctor.
I showed up scruffy the next day, and they called me terrorist.
I grew out my beard, and they called me maharishi.
I left a goatee, and they called me Rushdie.
I cleaned it up into a mustache, and they called me fresh off the boat.
I got rid of the mustache, and they called me doctor again.
So tell me, I said, what brings you in today?
What is bothering you?
What keeps you up at night?

Replacement Fertility (II)

When the roundups stop, you and your beloved discover, to your surprise, that you have survived. The authorities are apologetic; mere harassment, the poking and tweaking that was going on for centuries, got out of hand. You and your beloved accept the fruit basket and set to work reburying the dead in individual graves.

When the work is done, you receive a letter from the authorities promising that you and your people will be spared, and indeed subsidized by the State, for the rest of your lives. The next roundups, the letter assures you, will occur a minimum of three generations from now and affect your great-grandchildren.

You and your beloved were planning on conceiving a child. You did not try in the attic, for obvious reasons; but you planned on trying as soon as your caloric intake returned to normal, which it has, ever since last Tuesday. This letter complicates matters. Lying side by side in the broken bed, hands folded on your stomachs like corpses at a wake, you and your beloved discuss the issue.

More roundups at some point in the future were always a possibility. In the letter, the authorities discuss it as a certainty. Yet your lives and the lives of your children (and of your grandchildren, if the letter is to be believed) are certain to be spared. If you refrain from bearing children, you will defy, from this chronological distance, those far-future roundups: You will snatch your descendants and hide them in nonexistence, safe from the secret police. By doing so, however, you will be colluding with the purpose of the roundups, which will be to exterminate your kind.

What if, instead, you have five more children than the one you intend? And exhort each of those children to have six children of their own? Six begetting six for three generations would create a multitude. Your people will require a tremendous amount of killing; you will have piled massive logistical difficulties on anyone daring to reinstitute the roundups.

Unless the technology of rounding up will have advanced proportionately by then, too. In which case you will have stocked a pantry for the beast.

You and your beloved wish you had some control in the matter. But you are already turning toward each other. Your bodies have decided for you.

Kill List

1. At a certain distance, it looks like a poem.
2. Transliterated, maybe, from the Arabic.
3. Short-lined.
4. Short-lived.
5. At a certain distance, it reads beautifully.
6. What its authors cultivate is anesthetic distance.
7. Don't think wreckage, think Brecht.
8. Warfare is the theater of detachments.
9. At a certain distance, an angry emperor becomes a god.
10. Distances are more certain now, thanks to satellites.
11. From the desert here to the desert there: 7252.86 miles.
12. At a certain distance, wing lights look like stars.
13. Cars look like Hot Wheels.
14. A human body looks like the stick figure in a game of Hangman.
15. We guess and fill in the blank of each letter.
16. When we make mistakes, line by line we construct the hanged man.
17. The hanged man represents the guesser.
18. The word in question may remain unknown at the end of the game.
19. The word can be a thing or a place.
20. Or a name.
21. At a certain distance, a kill list could be any kind of list.
22. Grocery.
23. Things to Do.
24. Top Ten.
25. Bucket.
26. When hanging a man, any distance between his body and the earth will suffice.
27. Just so long as he cannot touch the ground by extending his feet.
28. Like a thief on tiptoe stealing into airspace.
29. The list is a poetic device much favored by the American poet Whitman.
30. Whitman was the first to establish that a body can be sung electric.
31. American prisons promptly switched to the electric chair.
32. This gave way in some states to the lethal injection.

33. Apparently, physicians wanted a piece of the execution business.
34. At a certain distance, it looked like vaccination.
35. In the same way two thousand volts looks like an orgasm.
36. Or a seizure.
37. Seizures, too, are of various kinds.
38. Drugs can be seized at the border.
39. Fugitives can be seized in motel rooms.
40. By the collar, or, failing that, the throat.
41. Moments, too, can be seized.
42. I seized this one, for example, to prepare a kill list in the form of a poem.
43. A kill list, like a poem, bears the signature of its compiler at the bottom.
44. After its lines are revised away, that one name will remain.
45. Your eye, scanning from above, will focus on it.
46. You will make certain assumptions about my ethnicity, my religion, my politics.
47. At a certain distance, I admit, I do look like an Arab.
48. Your pupils will constrict, like a Predator's faced with a flashlight.
49. I have been waiting here for you, on the floor of this room.
50. *As-salamu alaykum.*

Everybody shows their wounds.
Look here, and here. They did us wrong.
Always their own, never the ones
their own inflict—as if those wounds
were somehow other than their own.
I, a Hindu, make this song
to show my own, to own those wounds.
Look there. Look hard. We did them wrong.

Godhra Sequence

[Gujarat, 2002]

The moon this night is a scythe
taken off its hook
and bobbing
above a crowd of men.

The moon will follow
anyone who walks her
anywhere, even me
into the hospital
where your pupils are new moons.

> *Qaidi, only the moon has a dark side.*
> *The sun is fire all the way around.*

If every call to prayer
is also a call for the dead,

no wonder by this moanlight
mosque and morgue
look like they might rhyme.

Hands to either side of his mouth,
a frenzied muezzin
is blowing on the sparks.

The fires catch.
The fires catch

us

doelike where we stand and listen,
turning to our futures.

      Qaidi, your eyes, too, are luminous.
      But not from within.

•

In the middle of a modern city,
they show up with farm tools.

Not just machetes, either.
Spades and shovels.

Murder full service,
burial included.

      Qaidi, she is thinking
      how absurd this schoolboy looks
      with garden shears

until the jab and
torque and
three quick jerks—

the legs
the handles
forced apart

ribs cracking
as the blades
work wide

the beet-red furrow that

invaginates her heart

•

Were you more afraid
of the police
with bamboo lathis
or the college boys
with hockey sticks
or the mechanic
with the crowbar?

What about the sticks
those small blunt
instruments
of theirs
hidden
and waiting
between their pockets?

Did running
from the matchsticks
only make you sweat
more kerosene?

Who rattled a twig
in this hive
of a city
calling out so many bees
with stingers cocked?

Qaidi,
you warrior
you too brandished a stick
in that city

a brittle twig
twisted off the Tree of Life
alive
its graphite pith
leeching language
from the gash in your neck

while a few blocks away
the chief minister
the chief monster
perfected his photogenic smile

with a toothpick

•

In North Carolina
on the television
in my brother's house

a silhouette
with an iPod
danced
against a background
hot pink

It took me back to Bali
and a shadow
puppet Rama
dancing

with grief and rage
on a backdrop
backlit
by an oil lamp
that a monkey
once kicked over
burning down the theater

Burning down
like Godhra
where my friend the lawyer
Shaukat Ehsan
is still dancing
in the flames
of his burning Fiat
while a mob of twenty thousand
whistle at his moves
clapping their hands
spinning their axes

> *Qaidi,*
> *if only we could hear the secret music*
> *of his pain*
> *we could spin with him*

·

I knew about the riots
the night before

when I started hearing
the fireflies
phosphoresce

click
click
click

all around me in the smog of dusk
that already stank of tires
not yet burning

click
click
click

like light switches
all across our city

I tried to warn you
making fists
and shutting my eyes
and trying as hard as I could

but at last when my fingernails
throbbed with a pink glow

six blocks east of me
rose that monstrous
firefly

the sun

·

We were not screaming, Qaidi

We were echolocating the silence

We were not running, Qaidi

We were tapping the pavement
with our feet
to see if it might give
like the trick floor
trapdoor
of a nightmare

We were not on fire, Qaidi

We were field testing
an experimental fabric
for wings

And when we crash-landed
and started moving our bony fingers
in the ashes
of our bodies

we were not drawing maps
to escape the city

not at all

we were drawing one another's faces

we were writing one another's names

•

When it was finished

the city
sloshed some traffic

over the spot
where my friend the lawyer
Shaukat Ehsan
burned

the city
scrubbed at the black stain
where the Fiat's tires melted
scrubbed
scrubbed it away
                        with Tata trucks
            bicycles
                                                    sandals
                    hoofs
paws
                                        rain

the city
bleached our whole neighborhood
with camera flashes

and hid the bodies
under the saffron tarpaulin
of a stage-managed
apologia

To this day, Qaidi,
the only scorch marks
are on my memories

branded with his initials
for life

cattle
chattel

property
of the dead

•

Memory, Memory

holy heifer

whose udder
every morning

I milk of pus

•

First of all, it was all true. Everything you saw.

You must trust your memory
no matter what the loudspeakers
mounted on those vans
are saying.

If you brush your skin
and paint comes off
keep rubbing
until you expose the purple
subcontinent
of the bruise.

> *What you saw was the truth, Qaidi.*
> *Anything else is the news.*

I slough my skin. I hatch. I molt.
Am I the me I was before?
I'm desperate, as I grow old,
to slip my bones, remodel, melt
these sleeves of selves that leave me cold.
Can what I was before transform?
Or do I, when I break my mold,
transform to what I was before?

A Natural History of the Jailbird

. . . So much for the natural history of the Crow.
As for its cousin, or stepbrother, or birth dad,
vertical stripes on the earliest jailbirds
served to blend them in with their cages.
They disappeared into their own blackness
like sons of night hunted at night
camouflaged against the night.
Over time, however, jailbirds evolved
a vivid coloring from top to toe
in a desperate attempt to be witnessed:
orange plumage nailed to the perch,
orange jumpsuit in search of a ledge.
Today's jailbirds, if released, would die
out in the wild, hunted to extinction
by their own kind. Their keepers agree
the jailbird should consider himself
a bird of paradise, because hell, what comes
before paradise but purgatory?
The jailbird's cell is papered with pages
of the dictionary. *Wing*, he learns,
never did mean what he thought it meant.
To injure in a manner that disables,
as by grazing with a bullet.
Every jailbird hides a bullet somewhere,
if only in his future, one that shatters
on entering his body, like a meteor
that breaks up as it penetrates
the atmosphere of night. Bone
is hard enough to shatter metal.
Of course the bone must shatter, too,

bone splinters, bullet fragments, spikeshine
star flares on a CT scan at midnight.
Another thing with wings is winged and grounded—
a jailbird, bleeding, bound in gentle gauze,
one more blackbird baked into the pie.

I Carceri

after Giovanni Battista Piranesi

1.

If the mind is one of those Piranesi prisons, she said, full of darkly nested
architectural redundancies—as we know the human brain is, with its neurons
like ropes slung precariously from cell to cell, and interrupted spiral stairwells
going neither up nor down, lions hinting at some tapestried past when all this
was a brighter castle—then God, for lack of a better word, and after all these
centuries we do lack a better word, at least in English, then God is a cricket
somewhere in that oppressively expansive complexity, or really just the cricket's
song stuck in your head, and it is up to you now, as the torches gutter, to find
out where that cricket's song is coming from so you can stomp it and go back
to sleep

2.

I like to rest my wrists, he said, like this, on the crossbar, so part of me hangs
outside my cell, in the hallway, because that is freedom, right there, and when
my fingers touch it, they are trailing over the side of a sailboat, unzipping a
depth I can daydream hiding in, though I know that plunging anything more
than a forearm into the water is impossible,

cat's-cradled in the complex rigging as my body is back here, with loops of rope
around my waist and arms and one loop more around my neck, this origami
sailboat folded from a deposition the district attorney produced from his
briefcase, this river the length of a sentence, this sentence the length of a life

3.

Because his mother, who stared too long at the sun, covered her forearms in
the bright red Braille of fire-ant stings, that untranslatable text the closest she

came to tenderness, he spent his boyhood waving his arms, trying to be seen by her, or anyone really,

but then those arms of his, bumping a brown kid in glasses, turned out, to his surprise, to have fists at the ends of them, fists that could connect with anyone at all,

the fight progressing rapidly to a waist-level arms-out charge-and-lunge that was his first embrace, the ring of fourth-graders that watched him beat me up the first eyes to see him, this new thrill of visibility so addicting him

that fourteen years later, he found his way to a house of watchers:

two guards, thumbs in belt, who oversee his shuffle through the slop line, his spotter on the bench press, suitors yearning through the shower steam, closed-circuit cameras in the corners, this home that will never neglect him, this family that will never let him go.

4.

Even if you could slip out of your cell, a cell irregularly polyhedral, as if your captivity increased with the number of walls, even if you could race through that Piranesi prison where you were fathered by a warden upon a madwoman in mismatched sneakers, even if you could tarzan the ladder-thick chains toward a rumor of daylight, and stab the oxycodone-groggy guards and gargoyles where they sprawl,

your wraithlike body would go poof at the first touch of raw sunlight, its fistful of talc cast on the breeze, and the prison's intake vents would swirl you back down into the very air of the prison, incorporated, part of the odor, one more thought in that giant unkillable brain.

Time

For each gram in the Ziploc bag, ten years.
He swallowed the time, but the time
was in his bloodstream after that,
like original sin. The time expressed
itself, but not in numbers, rather, in a sentence
whose syntax kept him in the passive voice,
the past tense ever after. On his irises
were hair-thin hour hands and minute hands,
left eye ticking clockwise, right eye stopped
at nineteen years old by a lightning strike
to his temple, a nightstick striking
midnight in his drug bust skull still ringing.
Oxycontin exiled him into a desert
for forty days and forty nights
and forty years and counting.
Moses, said the chaplain, was allowed to see
the Promised Land but not to enter it.
The inmates are permitted television.
A smuggled chalk bit line line line line
slashes years—so many little cages
for hummingbirds that do not live long
in captivity. Their rapid heart rates keep them
on the move; they have no time. *Be patient,*
says the prophet of chicken finger Fridays,
so he splashes his face a few more times,
convincing his circadian rhythm
this sunlessness may yet become a morning.
The dealer, like his drug, has a half-life.
Instead of marking time, he draws an orchid
and waits for hummingbirds to come and sip,
the chalk bit breaking up against the brick
and white the powder sweetening his fingers.

What He Did in Solitary

Named all the state capitals

Sang as much of *The Miseducation of Lauryn Hill* as he had tattooed on his eardrums, which was all of it

Tugged, instead of magician's scarves, blinking Christmas lights from somewhere deep inside him

And strung them in spirals up and down his prison bars

Realized Edmond Dantès, in the Chateau d'If, was imprisoned in the Castle of Possibility

Listed the five best Mexican places he'd eaten at

Thought hard about the first love he ever touched until the scent reappeared on his index and middle

Pared his nails with his teeth and kept going until he bled

Used the blood to paint the butterfly from *Papillon* on his breastbone

Laid his ear on different parts of the floor and walls to see if footsteps or earthquakes might transmit from somewhere

Plugged the drain with two fistfuls of hair and filled the sink with water because every garden walling in an innocent should have a birdfeeder

Played with himself

Lost interest

Listed all the Presidents

Palmed his scalp to feel his hair grow

Thumbed his eyelids up so his helium-filled eyeballs could float out of their sockets on yellowish neural tethers

Scraped the bricks with his teeth to fill his navel with brick grit so that one of his fingernails, potted, might grow into a hand

Did a hundred squats

Imagined himself in his boyhood's public library so hard the bricks became the spines of Tolkien novels stacked to the ceiling

Hunted the corners and under the cot for a spider to talk to

Monologued mightily, making appeals to logic and mercy that would have gotten him acquitted

Prayed, hands together, on his knees, for deliverance from his own company

Shouted at the ceiling

Took a deep breath, pursed his lips, pinched his nose, and blew out, bursting both tympanic membranes with a sound so gunshotlike it reminded him of home

Made shapes with his tongue in the mirror until his tongue, finally, after hundreds of attempts, forked

Stood on his hands until he got a headache

Sobbed

Realized he'd left out John Tyler and listed all the Presidents again

Whistled and patted his thighs as if his beagle Ben were running back to him

Spoke both parts in a stage play of his own making about the Rodney King riots

Lunged at the Saran-wrapped sandwich slid through the slit in his cell door, hoping hungrily to glimpse his jailor's human hand

Congratulated himself on making it to lunch

Peeled the Saran wrap off the sandwich

Ate

What He Dreamed in Solitary

A windowless shed the size of an airplane hangar where birds were bred flightless

Twenty treadmills in a row and twenty rich men running

His old house in East Cleveland, seen from the backseat cage of a slowing cop car, his mom sitting on the lawn

And she got up and rushed to him arms out but her choke chain jerked taut

A prayer rug made of flowing water

A kufi made of his brother's caul

Bees crawling in and out of the windows of Terminal Tower

His brother, fetal position, kicked by six cops, but his clever body smoking into its own atoms all around them, rising like dust beaten from an old mattress

His old house in East Cleveland with the snow on its roof dyed the color of rocket ice by cop car lights

A prison island off the coast of Sweden where murderers were whittling owls and rapists were doing collages

A state-of-the-art walkway over an abyss, its floor made of one long glass screen that showed the drop below it

Twenty lounge chairs in a row and twenty rich girls sunning

Him dressed in boy shorts and ankle shackles, balancing their wine coolers on a tray, forbidden to sip

The old house in East Cleveland with his brother sitting astride the roof in a captain's hat, face to the wind, excelsior

A concrete mixer with bodies mixed in, pouring a public sculpture where the bodies, trying to emerge, harden into place in attitudes of anguish grasping skyward

Twenty rich couples strolling their kids through this park to teach them about civil rights

And him equipped with nothing but a hammer and a pen, checking the faces of these figures for his brother

Until the light changes and the concrete bodies softening to marble become those unfinished sculptures of Michelangelo known as *The Prisoners*

Only they aren't emerging, they're returning to their blocks

As he is now, a catnap Rip Van Winkle, twenty minutes and his beard is past his knees

Awakening in solitary yet again

What He Drew in Solitary

An occult chalk outline of his brother on the floor, a gap where his mouth
should have gone, for black ants to file through like song notes

Illustrations for a pop-up book for blinded boys, you turn the page and run
your fingers airily along a wall

Crooked white fences between himself and despair, four finger-length
fenceposts and a cross slash, repeated all the way around

A single eye on a single brick, his brother keeping watch through an
observation slit

Dashed lines of a flea-flicker from John Madden Football they played as boys

One of those dashed lines wandering off toward the ceiling, X marks the spot

A treasure map from the Chateau d'If to the island of Only

Shin-high sunflowers seed-stippled with Vicodins

A sun for those sunflowers, too, so ghostly pale it turned into a moon at night

And made the water level in the toilet bowl subside and rise in tides

A shin-high cross beside the dead-end road where boyhood crashed, killing his
brother, leaving him the sole survivor

Cursed to grow into a grown man slack-limbed on a prison cot

Quadriplegic, unable to stand, unable to stand this

Wanderlust butane-torching ulcers in his flesh

While lust expresses, expels itself in chalk-dust teardrops on his palm

Drawing him deeper into self-erasure, gaunt body, hunted skin, drawn face

Illuminating the scripture of his solitude, in which there is only one God, one way

And that way, inward

To the fund of images he draws on, replenished every evening by a distant indulgent father

Making up for his longlostness with these lengths of chalk, these drawings in the dark

Basilica Basquiats in his brother's nightstick-fractured skull

Exposed to sunlight by a pipe bomb laid in his boy body's inviolate Vatican

Illustrations, lustrations in the cloister, bare back Jackson-Pollocked with a penitential whip

Here in his cell, in solitary, fighting himself to a draw

Drawing sustenance, drawing from the well, drawing his family like a treasure map from memory, drawing in the face of faces turned away forever

Breath

Breath

Breath

Permissions Acknowledgments

The author wishes to thank the editors of the following publications, in which these poems first appeared:

32 Poems: "Detachment," "How Do I Say That, Where Is That From," "Rigidity," "Virus"

Able Muse: "The Compass Rose"

America: "His Vision," "Kicking the Can Down the Road," "Neurology of Love," "Tripping on Metaphors," "The Weaver's Song"

Arion: "Four Ways of Looking at Argus," "Observing Orpheus"

Arkansas International: "Chillicothe Apostrophe"

Awl: "Apocalypse Shopping List"

Best American Poetry 2017: "Kill List"

Chicago Quarterly Review: "1979"

The Cincinnati Review: "The Colony" [from "Reverse Colonization"], one poem from "I Carceri" ["If the mind is one of those Piranesi prisons"]

Cog: "Bloodline," "Innocents Abroad"

Dark Horse: "Rate Your Pain"

Diode: "Neuroastrogenesis"

Ecotone: "Elemental," "The Fencing Shoe," "To His Soul," "The Turin Horse," "Visionary Sonzal" "Solitary Sonzal"

FIELD: "Ode to a Jellyfish"

First Things: a selection from "Letters to Myself in My Next Incarnation" ["The peak that paints the lake"]

Free Verse: "I Carceri," "Casus Belli"

Granta Online: "The Adventures of Amit Majmudar"

Hopkins Review: "Bully" [winner, Pushcart Prize, 2018], "The Plague Comes to Bologna," a selection from "Letters to Myself in My Next Incarnation," selections from "Godhra Sequence"

Image: "Altarpiece," "The Smithsonian Museum of Supernatural History"

Juxtaprose: "A Natural History of the Jailbird"

Kenyon Review Online: "Resurrection: His Hands"

Literary Matters: "Combat," "Deaths of the Eminent Philosophers," "The Pediatric Cardiothoracic Surgery Floor," "The Rumi Variations"

Magma: "Replacement Fertility (I)"

Massachusetts Review: "Invasive Species" [winner, Anne Hawley Prize, 2019], "Vocative"

The Midnight Oil: "Why an Octopus"

Modern Age: "The Syndrome"

The Nation: "Kill List"

The New Criterion: "The Bear," "Theory of Incompleteness"

New Ohio Review: "The Potter's Field"

New Poetry from the Midwest: "Apocalypse Shopping List," "Grooming"

The New Yorker: "The Beard," "Of Age"

Oxford Poetry: "Reverse Colonization"

The Paris Review: "Nostalgia"

Plume: "Letters to Myself in My Next Incarnation," selections from "Godhra Sequence"

Poetry International: "The Plague Comes to Bologna," "The Weaver's Song," selections from "Godhra Sequence"

Poetry Northwest: "The Irreversible Spread of the Gypsy Moth"

River Styx: "Elmer's Glue," "Grooming," "Owed to Cleveland"

Shenandoah: "What He Did in Solitary," "What He Dreamed in Solitary," "What He Drew in Solitary" (under the title "Prison Suite")

Valparaiso Poetry Review: "Autumnal," "Elegy with van Gogh's Ear," "Squanderlust"

Word Riot: "Replacement Fertility (II)"

The poet owes a special debt of gratitude to his agent, Georges Borchardt; to Deborah Garrison and Todd Portnowitz, who saw this manuscript through its many-minded metamorphoses; and to the late Sonny Mehta.

A NOTE ABOUT THE AUTHOR

Amit Majmudar is a diagnostic nuclear radiologist who lives in Westerville, Ohio, with his wife and three children. His latest works are *Dothead,* his third poetry collection, and *Godsong: A Verse Translation of the Bhagavad-Gita, with Commentary.* He is also the editor of the anthology *Resistance, Rebellion, Life: 50 Poems Now.* Awarded the Donald Justice Poetry Prize and the Pushcart Prize, Majmudar's work has appeared in numerous publications, including *The New York Times, The New Yorker, The Best of the Best American Poetry,* and the eleventh edition of *The Norton Introduction to Literature.* He blogs for the *Kenyon Review* and is also a critically acclaimed novelist.

A NOTE ON THE TYPE

This book was set in Scala, a typeface designed by the Dutch designer Martin Majoor (b. 1960) in 1988 and released by the FontFont foundry in 1990. While designed as a fully modern family of fonts containing both a serif and a sans serif alphabet, Scala retains many refinements normally associated with traditional fonts.

Composed by North Market Street Graphics,
Lancaster, Pennsylvania

Printed and bound by LSC/Harrisonburg,
Harrisonburg, Virginia

Designed by Soonyoung Kwon